D0417646

BLACKWORK

A New Approach

BLACKWORK

A New Approach

BRENDA DAY

Guild of Master Craftsman Publications Ltd

First published 2000 by
Guild of Master Craftsman Publications Ltd,
166 High Street, Lewes,
East Sussex, BN7 1XU

© Guild of Master Craftsman Publications Ltd

Reprinted 2000, 2001

ISBN 1 86108 148 0

Project chapter photographs and cover photograph by Chris Skarbon

Ilustrations by John Yates from sketches by Brenda Day

Charts, patterns, some sketches and photographs in
'Getting started with your own designs' produced by Brenda Day

All rights reserved

The right of Brenda Day to be identified as the author of this work has been asserted
in accordance with the Copyright Designs and Patents Act 1988, Sections 77 and 78.

No part of this publication may be reproduced, stored in a retrieval system, or
transmitted in any form or by any means without the prior permission of the
publisher and copyright owner.

This book is sold subject to the condition that all designs
are copyright and are not for commercial reproduction without the
written permission of the publisher and copyright owner.

The publishers and author can accept no legal responsibility for
any consequences arising from the application of information, advice
or instructions given in this publication.

A catalogue record of this book is available from the British Library.

Design and cover design by Angela Neal

Typeface: Bembo

Colour origination by Viscan Graphics (Singapore)
Printed by Sun Fung Offset Binding Co Ltd, China

This book is dedicated to my mother, Sarah Glover,
who sadly died during its preparation.

ACKNOWLEDGEMENTS

My thanks are due to Fabric Flair, DMC Creative World Ltd, Framecraft,
Glyn Owen, Craft Creations and Macleod Craft Marketing for their unstinting help in
providing materials for the projects in this book; to Martin Lawson-Smith of I L Soft,
for guiding me through the quagmire of computer programmes; to Angela Wigglesworth for
allowing us to use her delightful B&B in Lewes to shoot the photography;
to my managing editor, Stephanie Horner, and very patient editor, Kylie Johnston;
and finally, to my family, particularly my husband, Charles, who encouraged
me and listened stoically throughout it all.

PICTURE ACKNOWLEDGEMENTS

pviii, The Bridgeman Art Library/Kunsthistorisches Museum, Vienna;
p1, Lindy Dunlop; p2, Lindy Dunlop;
p3, The Bridgeman Art Library/Kunsthistorisches Museum, Vienna;
p4, Mary Cornwallis by George Gower, © Manchester City Art Galleries;
p6, V&A Picture Library; p7, V&A Picture Library; p96 (Soay ram), National Trust Photographic Library;
p98, Lindy Dunlop; p99, Jerry Harpur/Harpur Garden Library.

CONTENTS

INTRODUCTION

When Catherine of Aragon arrived in England in 1501 to wed Prince Arthur, eldest son of King Henry VII, her trousseau contained several items of 'Spanish work of black silk'.

Faire Katherine, Daughter to the Castile King,
Came into England with a pompous traine
of Spanish Ladies, which she thence did bring.
She to the eight King Henry married was
And afterwards divorc'd, where vertunsly
(Although a Queene) yet she her dayes did passe,
In working the Needle curiously,
As in the Towre, and place more beside,
Her excellent memorials may be seene:
Whereby the Needles prayse is dignifide
By her fair Ladies, and herseilfe, a Queene...

JOHN TAYLOR
THE NEEDLE'S EXCELLENCY, 1636

A LITTLE TUDOR HISTORY

When Catherine of Aragon arrived in England in 1501 to wed Prince Arthur, eldest son of King Henry VII, records show that her trousseau contained several items of 'Spanish work of black silk'. These beautifully embroidered items reflected not only the Spanish style and Catherine's love of needlework, a skill and a passion she inherited from her mother, but secured her place in embroidery myth. The legacy of this myth persists today, begging the question: did Catherine introduce blackwork to England, or did she simply popularize a vibrant, new style of a much older craft?

The Spanish blackwork style has its roots in North Africa. Spain was ruled by the Moors for eight centuries until their final overthrow in 1492 and during their long reign the Moors influenced all aspects of Spanish life, including artistic and architectural forms. One only has to look at the

Fig 2a. Example of Moorish architecture at the Alhambra, Granada

intricate, interlacing patterns which are a feature of the Alhambra in Granada to see how easily they were translated into embroidery. The Islamic preoccupation with symmetry and the use of geometric motifs and all-over patterns is very apparent (Figs 2a & b), while more naturalistic forms, because of their religious exclusion, are not.

It is less easy to pinpoint the origins of the English blackwork style. They may be Moorish, although various forms are also known from the Slavonic countries of Eastern Europe. Although no examples remain, the craft evidently pre-dates the Tudor period, for in Geoffrey Chaucer's 'The Miller's Tale', written between 1388 and 1400,

Fig 1. Michiel Sittow's portrait of Catherine of Aragon

Fig 2b. Example of Moorish tile at the Alhambra, Granada

Fig 3. Hans Holbein's portrait of Jane Seymour. Note the elaborate stitching on the cuff of her sleeve

Alison, the carpenter's wife, is described thus:

> *Her smock was white; embroidery repeated*
> *Its pattern on the collar front and back,*
> *Inside and out; it was of silk and black.*

From Chaucer's *Canterbury Tales* we can only deduce that blackwork was presumably widely used, even by the working classes, and wonder what form it took. It is impossible to ascertain the history of blackwork before this period because, as many writers have noted, although stone, brass and other memorials depict decorative patterns on clothing, it is difficult to distinguish between lace and embroidery.

It seems likely that Catherine's passion for beautiful, decorative needlework reinvigorated and popularized an already established form of embroidery. Ladies at court must have noted and emulated Catherine's choice of household linen, sheets and pillow covers, as well as her embroidered garments. The influence of royalty on fashion is prevalent today and so it was in Tudor times.

This, then, was the basis from which it seems English blackwork grew and eventually developed into the flowing, leafy designs, of which fine examples still survive.

The early Tudor examples were worked in double running stitch, or Holbein stitch as it became known, because of its appearance in the many portraits by Hans Holbein the Elder (1465–1524) and his son, Hans Holbein the Younger (1497–1543). The latter's portraits of King Henry VIII and of Henry's wife, Jane Seymour (Fig 3), show fine examples of blackwork of the period, with the formal arabesques and geometric patterns reproduced in detail. One of the best examples of this period, however, is George Gower's portrait of Mary Cornwallis, dated 1573, whose sleeves, cuffs and gown display a complex, intertwining pattern of oak leaves, lilies and roses (Fig 4). Portraits by other European artists of the same period confirm that this fashion was not unique to England.

Beautiful examples of the later, more naturalistic style of the Tudor period have survived and are held in collections around the world, particularly in Britain and America (see Sources of Information, page 100). That there are not more examples can simply be accounted for by the fact that the storage of clothing was not a priority in Tudor times. Soap, which was first home-made in the fourteenth century, must also have contributed to the destruction of many beautifully worked fabrics. It is hard for us to imagine laundering clothes with soap made from cow-dung, hemlock, nettles and refuse!

Such a mixture, and the effect of time, might well account for the fact that some surviving blackwork examples are not black, but brown.

THE PRODUCTION OF BLACKWORK

The name 'blackwork' refers to the fact that the embroidery was usually worked with black silk thread, most of which was imported via the Netherlands, for silk production in England did not develop until the seventeenth century. Originally, dyes for silk which could be made up at home were prepared from tannins of oak galls or the sumac tree and from salts of iron. Many such dyes were not colourfast, another contributory factor to the brown blackwork. Some examples departed from the traditional Spanish use of black silk and were worked in red or green, but black was generally the order of the day. Today's embroiderer deviates in a number of ways from the traditional blackwork, but predominantly in the use of colour – often using a negative image. The later Tudor blackwork featured a hard outline of stitches containing a pattern, but these have now given way to softer edges formed by the pattern itself.

Spangles, very similar to our present-day sequins, were often used to embellish blackwork. Originating in Italy, these were made from thin sheets of silver gilt cut into small circles with a hole pierced through the centre. Similarly, modern blackworkers often use beading and sequins to add a gleam and sparkle to their work.

The needle was (and still is) the embroiderer's most essential item. In the Tudor period, they were made either of drawn wrought iron which was not very durable, or, preferably, of steel which was hard and resilient. Those made of the latter were known as sprior needles and were highly valued. Very often, they were so costly to manufacture that a small community might possess only one. Pins were also expensive. Made in two parts with the head soldered to the shank, a day's output would number only twenty. It has been suggested that the expression 'pin money' derives from the length of time required to save for them.

FABRICS FOR BLACKWORK

Both clothes and household articles in the sixteenth century were made of linen, ranging from 'lawn', a very fine, semi-transparent cloth named after the French town of Laon, to 'lockram' which was much coarser. The wealthy English classes used a huge amount of linen and although much was home-produced, still more had to be imported, particularly the fine qualities from France. Linen was produced from the flax *Linum usitatissimum*, the stalks of which were retted, dried, crushed and beaten to produce linen thread which was very strong and durable. The range of dyes available in this period was limited so linen thread was bleached pure white, forming a strong contrast to the fashionable blackwork. The fine weave of lawn requires a great deal of work and is, therefore, very seldom used by the present-day stitcher in favour of fabrics such as Aida and evenweave cottons. Linen, on the contrary, is much favoured today because of its availability in a range of colours and evenweave form which produces patterns of great accuracy. Cotton was not generally used in any quantity until the late sixteenth century with the defeat of the Spanish Armada and the establishment of the British East India Trading Company which meant that raw cotton, rather than the spun fibre, became available. Linen nonetheless remained and continues to remain, the first choice for blackwork.

INSPIRATIONS AND DESIGNS

As we have seen, the formal arabesques and geometric patterns which are the hallmark of Arabic work in Spain gradually gave way in English blackwork to scrolling, more naturalistic designs and variations in texture were achieved with the use of stitches such as coral, satin, herringbone and buttonhole (Fig 5). A few examples feature a plaited braid stitch worked in metal threads. As the motifs became more varied, some tended to the rather freakish: a bodice known as the Falkland tunic in London's Victoria & Albert Museum collection, displays a range of mythic figures, fantastical animals and creatures such as the griffin (Fig 6). More generally, the coiling designs depicted the familiar

Fig 4. George Gower's portrait of Mary Cornwallis

Fig 5. Late sixteenth-century grape pattern worked on a pillow cover. The embroideress has used a range of stitches including backstitch, chain stitch and buttonhole stitch

flowers and herbs of the Tudor knot garden and herb garden, including roses, pansies, honeysuckle and comfrey.

The change in style relates historically to the period of transition between the end of the Middle Ages and the beginning of Renaissance England, a change which is evident in all art forms, particularly architecture, where the ornamental strapwork and scrolling are typical of the exuberant Elizabethan interpretation.

The development of sixteenth century embroidery owed much to the appearance of the first pattern books. The invention of printing in the mid-fifteenth century transformed the scene and by 1500 scribes were no longer required. In England, the aristocracy commissioned books from William Caxton, whose first printing press ran in this country in 1476. Many books were imported from the Continent, although these were usually in Latin. In later books the same illustrations reappear, so we can only imagine that the block maker travelled with them or sold them abroad, or else copied whatever took his fancy.

The earliest pattern books contained little text apart from the title page and the illustrations were

usually woodcuts which, being printed in black on a white page, provided a ready source of design material for the stitcher. Herbals, which included illustrations of the plants used in their recipes, and bestiaries, with their illustrations of strange animals and birds from far-off lands, as well as books such as *Aesop's Fables*, gave the needlewoman further material from which to select motifs. Wallpapers and lining papers of the late sixteenth century, also printed from wood blocks, offered another source of design inspiration. These papers were used to line chests and desks and while some are based on diaper patterns, others show English birds and butterflies as well as floral, fruit and heraldic motifs.

The first embroidery pattern book to be published in England, in 1548, was engraved on copper by a surgeon named Thomas Geminus. Only one copy now exists of *Moryssche & Damaschin renewed & encreased very profitable for Goldsmiths and Embroiderars*. Very early examples of pattern books are rare, as the actual pages of the books had to be pricked during the transference of the design to the fabric, a process known as 'prick and pounce', where the outline of the design was pricked very regularly with a needle before pounce powder (made from charcoal and cuttlefish bone) was pushed through the holes onto the fabric. This left a dotted line which could then be joined up with a fine ink line drawn with a quill. The technique is still used today for some forms of embroidery, minus the quill, of course! By the end of the sixteenth century designs were being printed directly onto the fabric from engraved plates.

Between 1501 when Catherine of Aragon married Prince Arthur and 1603 when Queen Elizabeth died, blackwork underwent a remarkable transformation. What started out as simple bands of decoration on the edges of garments, developed into the exuberant, foliar forms of the Elizabethan era, a development which can be directly related to parallel developments in such diverse fields as architecture, calligraphy, communications and printing.

MODERN BLACKWORK

With the advent of the Stuart period, the use of traditional black silks gave way to coloured silks and fabrics. This was largely a response to developments in art, fashion and technology. The needlewoman relied less on the stark contrasts typical of the Tudor period, than on the subtle use of shading and colour. Thereafter, blackwork in its purest sense virtually ceased to exist in England until the advent of the Arts and Crafts movement at the beginning of the twentieth century which sought to revive traditional craftsmanship. A number of key texts appeared in the 1920s and 30s, most notably *Samplers and Stitches* by Grace Christie, published in 1929. The proliferation of art school courses on the subject encouraged broader interest, and forms of embroidery that had almost been forgotten have, as a result, once again been made accessible to present-day stitchers.

In other parts of the world, however, blackwork evolved in different ways. In America, for example, blackwork enjoyed a resurgence in interest in the nineteenth century, although blue thread was often substituted for the traditional black and was probably influenced by the popularity of Delft tiles imported from Holland. In many countries throughout Eastern Europe, red thread was very popular and this

style continues to be worked in many countries. All over the world, variations on blackwork have evolved out of local customs and traditions, landscapes and influences, from as far apart as Australia, New Zealand, Russia and South Africa.

Embroiderers today use blackwork in a very modern way, basing their work on the contrast of stitch and background which is an integral part of its appeal, combined with a more liberated approach to design and function.

In the projects which follow, I have used many of the counted thread patterns from the Tudor period, as well as a variety of stitches. Some designs, for example the mirror frame, are based upon traditional designs and others, like the sheep panel, push the limits of the technique well beyond that envisaged by the Tudor needlewoman. If you have not tried blackwork before, start with a charted design before you attempt one of the more complex projects.

I hope that you have as much fun stitching these projects as I did designing them and that once you have developed a little confidence, you will design many of your own!

Fig 6. This detail of the Falkland tunic features a rather curious griffin and warrior-like lion

MATERIALS AND EQUIPMENT

For the techniques used in this book, very little is needed in the way of equipment.
As you progress and tackle more complex designs you will need to add to your range of
threads, fabrics and other items.

❖ Selection of tapestry, beading and
  sharps needles
❖ Fine-pointed embroidery scissors
❖ Dressmaker's scissors
❖ Roller or hand-held rectangular frames
  (available in a variety of sizes)
❖ Thimble
❖ Ruler
❖ Good quality white tissue paper
❖ Thread for tacking
❖ Good quality dressmaker's pins
❖ Iron

FABRIC

The best fabrics for blackwork are closely woven evenweave fabrics of cotton or linen with easily counted threads. The count relates to the number of threads or blocks to the inch, which in turn governs the size of the blackwork patterns. For the projects in this book I have used the following fabrics:

◆ Aida is a 100% cotton blockweave available in a variety of counts from 11 to 18. It is a very flexible fabric, available in a variety of colours including a version with lurex thread woven into it, which produces a striking effect. Many ready-made items are available with Aida panels in them, such as aprons and handtowels, which are wonderful to make up for the home and as gifts.

◆ Brittney is 52% cotton and 48% rayon, giving it a softer texture than Aida. It can be substituted for

14 count Aida and when stitched over two threads gives a more even surface.

◆ Jobelan is a 28 count fabric, usually worked over two threads and can be substituted for 14 count Aida.

◆ Jubilee is a 28 count 100% cotton fabric, particularly suitable for table linens and any article which may require frequent laundering.

◆ Linda is a 27 count 100% cotton evenweave fabric, closely woven. It drapes very well and has an easy-care finish.

◆ Oslo is a 22 count mercerized cotton, hardanger fabric which has a lustrous, silky appearance, making it suitable for a range of uses.

◆ Linen is available in a range of thread counts from 19 to 55 and is the traditional choice for blackwork.

A NOTE ON MEASUREMENTS

Some materials used in blackwork are only sold in metric units while others are commonly sold in imperial measures and although the fabrics are now sold in metres, they are still described in terms of 'holes per inch', or hpi. Throughout, measurements are given in both imperial and metric systems. Please use only one system for each project. The following conversion table may be useful.

11 squares per inch = 43 squares per 10cm
14 squares per inch = 55 squares per 10cm
16 squares per inch = 63 squares per 10cm
18 squares per inch = 71 squares per 10cm
22 squares per inch = 87 squares per 10cm

CONVERSION CHART FOR STRANDED THREADS

As you work your way through the projects in this book you will notice that I use DMC stranded threads which are available in a dazzling range of colours. If you cannot find a specific DMC thread, or prefer to use an alternative brand, please substitute. To help you, please refer to the following conversion chart, listing every DMC thread used in the projects and its Anchor equivalent.

DMC	Anchor	DMC	Anchor	DMC	Anchor
208	98	553	98	938	381
221	897	610	889	958	187
310	403	699	923	959	186
315	1019	701	227	961	76
317	400	720	326	991	1076
318	399	747	158	995	410
327	101	791	178	996	433
333	119	796	134	3021	905
355	1014	798	146	3022	8581
413	401	799	145	3350	59
414	400	824	164	3371	382
415	398	830	277	3740	872
435	365	832	907	3768	840
469	267	895	1044	3799	236
500	683	924	851	3812	188
502	876	926	850	3816	876
535	401	935	862	5200	1
550	101	937	268	Blanc	2

CONVERSION CHART FOR THREADS OTHER THAN STRANDED

DMC	Anchor
Perlé size 3	Size 3
Perlé size 8	Size 8
Perlé size 12	Coton à broder size 12
Coton à broder size 16	Size 16
Coton à broder size 25	Size 25
Metallic stranded thread	Lamé (two strands for every one of DMC): Gold 300, Silver 301
Soft embroidery thread	2926, 850, 2924, 851

Designs can differ greatly depending on the fabric count you choose. If you work on a 22 count fabric your design will appear more dense than if you work on a 14 count fabric. As you progress, you may wish to experiment with the count size, though it is best to practise first on a small piece of fabric. Keep in mind that altering the scale will also affect the quantities of thread you require.

EMBROIDERY THREADS

Threads are available in a wide range of colours and textures. Some are used as a single thickness (a thread which cannot be separated into strands), while others are composed of six strands which can be separated and rejoined in different proportions. To prevent excessive friction on your thread, it is best to restrict its length to no longer than 18in (450mm). Additionally, the thread should sit happily on the fabric without distorting its structure, so work small sample areas before embarking on a larger piece. The following threads are suitable for blackwork and have been used throughout this book:

- Stranded cotton, or 'silks', is normally available in skeins 8yd 2ft (8m) in length in an extensive range of colours. It is a six-strand thread with a slight sheen and is very adaptable.
- Perlé cotton is a two-ply thread which is more lustrous than stranded cotton and cannot be split. It comes in four sizes: 3, 5, 8 and 12.
- Coton à broder is a single thickness thread, softer than stranded or Perlé cotton and not as lustrous. It is available in a range of sizes.
- Caron Wildflowers is a single-strand, hand-dyed cotton, in variegated or space-dyed colours. The shading of these skeins is beautiful and it is tempting to let them overwhelm your work, so try to exercise a little restraint!
- Metallic embroidery floss is a six-strand metallic thread which can be split in the same way as stranded cotton and is about the same weight.

There are many other threads available and it is worthwhile having a look at the selection and experimenting with a few. There are various weights of machine threads, single-strand metallic threads and combinations of cotton and metallic threads.

NEEDLES

There are many types of needles and each performs a slightly different function. Although they are, to some degree, interchangeable, it is advisable to use the appropriate needle for a task.

- Tapestry needles for counted stitches have a large eye and blunt end which separates the threads of the fabric instead of splitting them. They are available in sizes 14–26.
- Sharps needles are, as their name suggests, fine and sharp-pointed, with a small eye. They are used for general sewing tasks such as hemming, and are available in sizes 3–10.
- Beading needles are very long and fine and used for attaching beads to an item. They are available in sizes 10–13. For the projects in this book a size 10 is adequate, but if you find the beading needle awkward to handle, you may find a size 10 crewel needle a good alternative.

Needles for blackwork have longer eyes than needles for plain sewing because they must accommodate thick threads or several thin ones. They are numerically graded from fine to coarse, the higher numbers being the finer needles.

Your choice of needle is a matter of preference, but the eye of the needle should accommodate the thread without difficulty and draw it through the fabric without distorting it. In the projects which follow, I tend to use either a size 24 or 26 tapestry needle for stitching. As a general rule, use a size 26 for working one strand of thread and a size 24 for two strands or a single thick thread. Once you have completed one or two projects you will soon be able to judge which size needle suits a particular task.

SCISSORS

It is a good idea to have two pairs of scissors: a large pair of dressmaker's scissors for cutting fabric and a small pair of embroidery scissors for cutting threads. To maintain your scissors and get the best results, it is best to use each for their appropriate tasks.

FRAMES

Roller frames are rectangular stitching frames, available in a variety of sizes from 12 to 36in (300–900mm) and essential for large, concentrated areas of stitching. The larger ones are supported on a floor-stand or can be propped against the edge of a table and enable the stitcher to control the tension and have both hands free to stitch. The smaller sizes are hand-held. Some embroiderers advocate the use of a ring or hoop frame, which consists of two rings, one fitting neatly inside the other. The fabric is positioned between the two rings which are then tightened together with a screw fitting to keep it taut and even. However, I would not recommend these frames for larger projects. They tend to trap stitches in the groove between the frames which can stretch and distort them.

You may find it easier to work smaller projects in your hand without the aid of a frame, but I always use one where the technique demands an even tension.

OPTIONAL ITEMS

Once you have been stitching for a while, you will find that some optional items make your work much easier. Some are very cheap to buy while others are more expensive, but that's fine – you can build up your range of accessories gradually.

If you stitch in a room with poor daylight, or only have time to stitch in the evening when it is dark, it is worth investing in an angle-poise lamp. Rather than the usual tungsten variety, use daylight bulbs. They have a blue coating which emulates daylight, enabling you to see the colour of your threads and fabrics in a more natural light.

I find a floss bobbin very useful, too. A floss bobbin is a piece of card or plastic with a slit in it; you wind your thread around the floss bobbin to keep it neat and tidy while you work, or to store half-used skeins of thread once you have finished a project.

Other useful items are magnifiers and metal chart stands. The former enables you to see your work more clearly and is available in different forms, while the latter enables you to keep abreast of your position on the chart without having to search for it.

There is nothing more satisfying than producing a good piece of work and then either mounting it or making it up as a cushion. You do not have to make up an item from scratch, however. There are a number of ready-made items on the market, ranging from towels to kitchen aprons with Aida band inserts ready to stitch. You will also find napkin rings and other smaller items which you can incorporate into your home or give to friends and family as gifts.

BASIC TECHNIQUES

Before you begin work on your embroidery there are a few basic techniques with which you need to be familiar, from preparing your fabric and tracing your designs to threading a needle — and this can be more difficult than you think! I hope that these guidelines will provide you with all the information you need to help you on your way.

PREPARING THE FABRIC

It is always worth spending a little time on the preparation of your chosen fabric before you begin to work your design. First, to remove any creases, press your fabric using a steam iron or, if you don't have one, a dry iron and a damp cloth. Next, cut the fabric to the size indicated in the instructions for the project and oversew the edges either by hand or machine to prevent fraying (Fig 7).

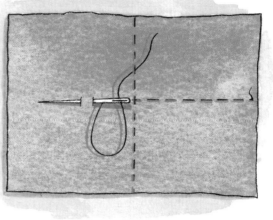

Fig 8

tacking stitches along both vertical and horizontal folds, using a thread which contrasts with the embroidery threads in your design so that you can remove it without difficulty (Fig 8).

Fig 7

MARKING THE CENTRE OF THE FABRIC

Charted Designs Begin by ensuring the design is centred on the fabric. To do so, fold the fabric in half and in half again. Form a crease where the two folds join and open out the fabric. Mark with a pin the point where both folds intersect and begin stitching there, relating your stitching to the centre of the chart. This method is satisfactory for small projects which can be worked in the hand. If the design is larger, use a tapestry needle and work a line of

Tacked Designs It is useful to tack your design if you are working a non-geometric design. Tack the vertical and horizontal folds as above, but use a different colour to tack the outline of the design. First, press a piece of good quality white tissue paper to remove any folds, then trace the vertical and horizontal lines on the drawing using a coloured pen. Trace the design itself with a contrasting colour. Lay the fabric onto a clean, flat surface and place the tissue paper with the traced lines on top, aligning the central lines on the tissue with the tack lines on the fabric. Working large stitches, tack the tissue to the fabric ½in (12mm) from the edge, ensuring that both are completely flat (Fig 9). If necessary, place a heavy weight on

Fig 9

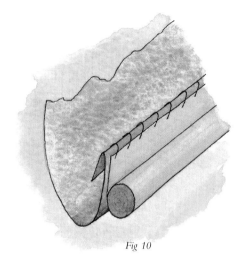

Fig 10

top of the tissue. Once flat, tack along the lines of the design with small stitches to preserve the shapes. As you stitch, ensure the fold lines always match. Begin each length of thread with a couple of overlapping stitches to ensure that it does not come loose and finish in the same way. Once you have transferred the whole drawing in this way, trim any loose ends, then very carefully tear away the tissue from around the tacked area of the design first and then from the centre. You are now ready to frame the fabric and begin stitching.

PREPARING A STITCHING FRAME

A stitching frame is essential when working on a large design because it helps you to stitch with a consistent, even tension. Begin by making a ½in (12mm) turning at the top and bottom edges of your fabric. Mark the centre of the edges and the centre of the webbing on both rollers. With right sides together, align these points and pin the fabric and webbing together. Starting from the centre and working outwards, stitch the fabric to the webbing using small, even overcasting stitches (Fig 10). Roll any surplus fabric onto the roller. Slot in the side pieces of the frame and tighten the screws to make your fabric taut. If your design is larger than the exposed area of fabric, it is advisable to trap a clean sheet of tissue paper between the layers of finished work as you roll it on. This prevents any damage to the work.

PREPARING THE THREADS

Stranded cotton has six strands which you will need to separate. Locate the end of the thread in the skein and, holding the skein at the band, pull gently on the thread until you have the required length, which should not be longer than 18in (450mm). If it is, the friction will produce an ugly, fluffy thread which will degrade the quality of the finished work. Now separate the strands of cotton. The best way to do this is to take the ends of the cut length in your fingers and gently pull apart. Separate each strand and assemble the required number (Figs 11a & b).

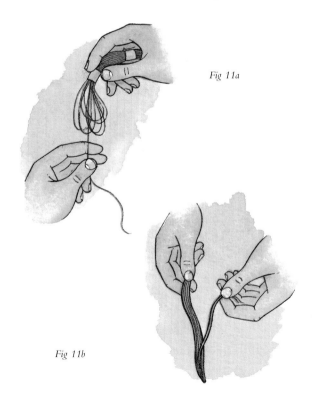

Fig 11a

Fig 11b

THREADING THE NEEDLE

A needle threader is useful, though not essential, for finer needles. Pass the wire loop through the eye of the needle, place the thread through the loop and draw the loop back through the needle eye, taking the thread with it. Alternatively, use the loop method. Loop the end of the thread around the needle and pull tightly. Slide the loop off the needle, nipping it tightly between your fingers, and push it through the eye of the needle (Fig 12).

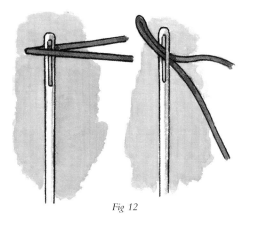

Fig 12

Threading the needle with metallic thread can be difficult. Flatten the end of the thread with a small piece of paper folded in half around it and push it carefully through the eye of the needle (Fig 13). Alternatively, you could follow the manufacturer's recommendations and knot the metallic thread with a slip knot through the eye of the needle to prevent it slipping (Fig 14). Use a needle one size larger than you would normally use to stretch the holes between the blocks or threads of the fabric, enabling

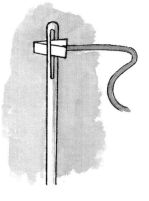

Fig 13

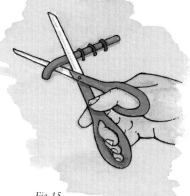

Fig 14

the metallic thread to pass through more easily.

When you are finally ready to stitch, you must secure your thread to the fabric. Do not make a permanent knot – this will leave an unsightly bump in the surface of your work. Instead, anchor the thread with a waste knot. Knot the end of the thread and, leaving the knot on the front of the work, insert your needle into an area which will be disguised by a blackwork pattern. This is particularly important if you are using a dark thread, as it may leave a mark where it pierces the fabric. Work an area of pattern until you reach the waste knot, cut it off, and complete the pattern. The thread which lies on the back of the work is now secured by the stitches of the pattern. Finish a thread by darning it securely into the back of existing stitches. When using a couching thread, leave a short length on the back of the work. Once you have finished couching, return to the loose end and secure it in place with one or two oversewing stitches, ensuring that they do not show on the front. Finish the end of your thread in the same way (Fig 15).

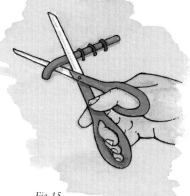

Fig 15

One of the joys of blackwork embroidery is that while there are many different stitches you can use to work your designs, there are few which are very difficult. With a little practice, you will soon be proficient.

Backstitch

Aside from being used to work blackwork patterns, backstitch is often used to outline a pattern and add definition. Following Fig 16, you first bring the needle up through the fabric a stitch-length along the line you wish to work. Then pierce the fabric with the needle at your starting point, drawing the thread through so that you now have a single, complete stitch. Finally, bring the needle up again through the fabric a stitch-length ahead of the last.

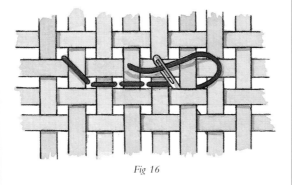

Fig 16

Your stitches should be neat and even in length. Backstitch is worked slightly differently depending on the fabric. With Aida, for example, each backstitch is worked along one side of a square, diagonally across the weave, or across two blocks of

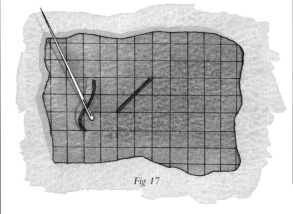

Fig 17

thread and one down (Fig 17) whereas the close weave of evenweave fabric demands that the stitch be worked across two threads.

Whipped backstitch

Whipped backstitch produces a slightly raised effect. Pass the whipping thread through each backstitch in turn, always through the same side and, apart from beginning and finishing off, you do not pass the needle through the fabric at all. It is best to first pass the eye end of the needle under each stitch to prevent the needle splitting either the backstitch itself or the background fabric (Fig 18).

Fig 18

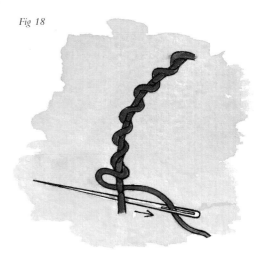

Holbein or double running stitch

Holbein stitch is the traditional stitch for blackwork embroidery. Its alternative name, double running stitch, is explained by its construction. You first stitch a row of running stitches, then make a return journey by working in between your original stitches (Fig 19). Occasionally you can work the stitches on the diagonal, but generally, follow the warp and weft of the fabric. This stitch works best on a regularly woven fabric because it is important for the stitch to remain regular, the same length on either side of the fabric.

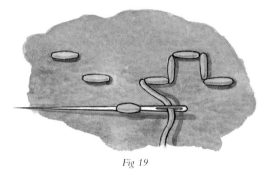

Fig 19

Couching

Couching is used to secure your thread to a piece of fabric, but it is also used for stitching an outline. You couch a thread by holding it down with a second, often finer thread by stitching small stitches at right angles over the first, like tiny bridges, to hold it in place, hence 'couching' the thread to the fabric (Fig 20). To achieve the best result, ensure these stitches are evenly spaced.

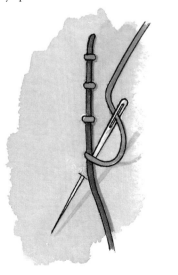

Fig 20

Cross-stitch

This is usually completed in two stages, particularly when working large areas. Stitch a row of diagonal stitches until you reach the end then return along the same row, stitching a reverse diagonal across the first. You can use this method horizontally or vertically, but always ensure the top arms of the crosses point in the same direction. This procedure is the same whether you are working on Aida or fine linen, except with Aida you work over one block of threads while with evenweave, you generally work over two threads of the fabric (Figs 21a & b).

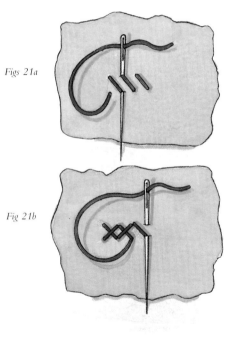

Figs 21a

Fig 21b

Chain stitch

Chain stitch produces a medium-thick, even stitch which is easy to manipulate around curves in a design. You bring the thread up through the fabric and then re-insert the needle at the same spot, bringing the point out a stitch-length ahead along the row. Take the thread under the needle-point in a simple loop. Pull the needle through and the thread re-emerges in a position to work the next stitch (Fig 22).

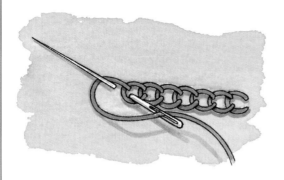

Fig 22

Fly stitch

Fly stitch is an open chain stitch. If you imagine a letter Y, draw the thread through at the top of the left-hand arm and insert it again at the top of the right-hand arm. Draw the needle through at the base of the V of the Y and pull it through over the working thread. Secure this loop with a straight stitch to form the leg of the Y (Fig 23).

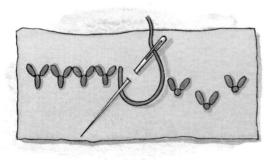

Fig 23

Herringbone stitch

This stitch is generally used for decorative borders, but can also be used as a filling-in stitch. You work this broad, open stitch by bringing the needle up through the back of the fabric at the top of a row, then taking it diagonally down to the bottom to form a complete diagonal stitch. Bring the needle up through the fabric a small stitch-length backward along the same row and take the thread diagonally across the first to form a broad, irregular cross.

Repeat the sequence as many times as necessary until you have a criss-cross network of stitches (Fig 24). Your chart will advise you of the correct spacing to follow.

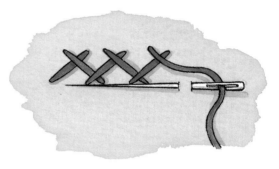

Fig 24

Pattern darning

This is basically a series of running stitches which is worked in rows and covers a set number of threads. For pattern darning, you generally work on an even, countable weave and on the warp or weft of the fabric, although occasionally you can work on the diagonal (Fig 25).

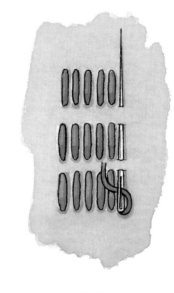

Fig 25

Slip stitch

This simple stitch is used to finish hems or close openings. Bring together the two edges of fabric you wish to join and stitch a line of small, diagonal stitches through both layers until the hem is completed or the opening sealed (Fig 26).

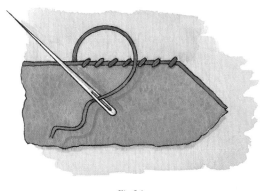

Fig 26

Ladder stitch

This stitch is also used to close openings, but without showing a trace of the stitch itself on the surface of the fabric. Following Fig 27, begin at one end of the opening in the two edges of fabric. Take a small stitch along the edge of the near piece of fabric, then a second along the edge of the far piece of fabric, so that the second stitch begins opposite the end of the first. Work several stitches in this way, pulling up the thread as you work so that the stitches disappear. Continue until you have a sealed seam.

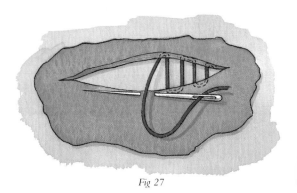

Fig 27

Compensation or partial stitch

This stitch is required when another element in the design interrupts the repeating pattern, for example an outline. The outline may be a stitched outline or a row of tacking which delineates the point at which the pattern finishes. The partial stitch brings the stitch used in the repeating pattern up to, but not beyond, the break at the outline. Always begin your repeating pattern from the centre of a shape so that the partial stitches are spread evenly around the edge (Fig 28). To ensure that the partial stitch lies at the correct angle, you may need to split a thread.

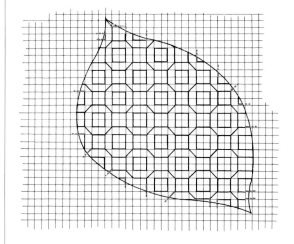

Fig 28

CHAPTER ONE

THE TRADITIONAL
BLACKWORK STYLE

The designs in this chapter are based upon the

natural forms and styles that inspired the Tudor

embroideress. They offer the beginner a gentle

introduction to traditional blackwork techniques, the

key feature of which is the repetition of small

patterns contained within bold outlines.

ROSE AND TULIP BOOKMARKS

The floral designs for these bookmarks are so simple and pretty, you might like to adapt them to other items: perhaps a special greetings card. Alternatively, select one aspect and use it as a motif for the border of a mirror frame, hand towel or curtain tie-back. Once you have experimented with the technique, you can adapt the designs to whichever item you choose.

SKILL LEVEL 1

DESIGN SIZE

2½ X 10IN (64 X 254MM)

STITCH COUNT

ROSE 23 X 116

TULIP 22 X 119

MATERIALS

**For each bookmark
you will need the following:**

White, 28 count Zweigart Jubilee, 13 x 4in (330 x 101mm)

White cotton for the backing, 13 x 4 in (330 x 101mm) (another piece of Jubilee will do)

Size 24 tapestry needle for the outline and size 26 for the pattern

Hand-held rectangular frame, small

Tacking cotton

Threads as listed in the colour key

WORKING THE DESIGN

1 Find the centre of the fabric by folding it into four, and mark it with a pin. Find the centre of the charted area by counting the squares and pencil a cross.

2 Attach the fabric to your frame (see Basic Techniques, page 14), ensuring that the fabric is pulled taut.

3 Count from the centre of the chart to the nearest point on the outline of the design and begin stitching at the same point on the fabric, using a single thickness of cotton Perlé to backstitch or sew double running stitch. Complete the whole outline before beginning the blackwork patterns in stranded cotton. You will need to work some compensation or partial stitches (see Basic Techniques, page 19).

4 When the embroidery is complete check for any mistakes, loose threads or areas which may have been soiled and then carefully press your work. If necessary, clean your work and press (see Finishing Techniques, page 83).

5 Cut a co-ordinating piece of fabric for the back of the bookmark and with right sides facing, tack the two pieces together (Fig 29).

6 Stitch along the tacked line, leaving a small opening in one long side. Remove the tacking, trim away the surplus fabric ¼in (7mm) from the stitching (Fig 30) and mitre the corners. You are ready to turn your bookmark right side out. Use ladder stitch to sew up the opening.

7 If you wish, add a pretty tassel to
the bottom of the bookmark using the
surplus Perlé cotton (see Finishing
Techniques, page 87).

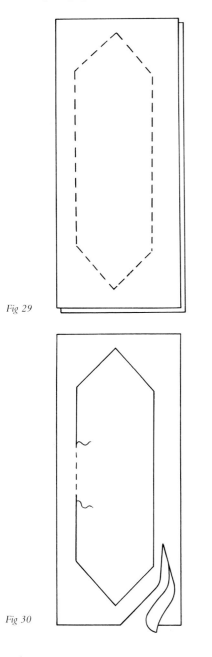

Fig 29

Fig 30

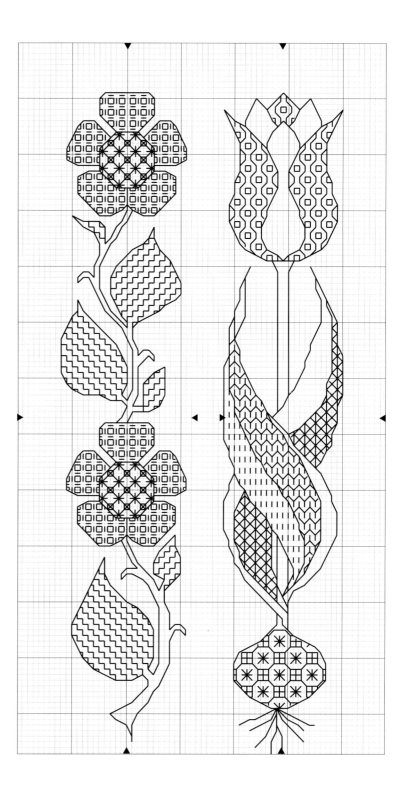

COLOUR KEY

	DMC Perlé	DMC Stranded	Size	Amount	Strands for backstitch	Strands for blackwork
▬	310		12	1 ball	1	
▬		310		1 skein		1 thickness

NB: each square on the chart represents 2 x 2 threads of the fabric.

GRAPEVINE MIRROR FRAME

This design was inspired by a famous blackwork cushion in London's Victoria & Albert Museum. Although I have adapted it to frame a mirror, it would suit any frame you wish to decorate. You might like to adapt the vine and leaf motif in other ways – perhaps for a matching placemat and napkin set for your dining room.

SKILL LEVEL 2

DESIGN SIZE

11½ X 11½IN (293 X 293MM)

FRAME CUT-OUT SIZE

4⅝ X 4⅝IN (118 X 118MM)

MATERIALS

Cream, 27 count Zweigart Linda (264), 14½ x 14½in (368 x 368mm)

Sheet of good quality white tissue paper, 14½ x 14½in (368 x 368mm)

Size 24 tapestry needle for the outline and size 26 for the pattern

Hand-held rectangular frame, 12 x 18in (300 x 459mm)

Tacking cotton

Threads as listed in the colour key

WORKING THE DESIGN

1 Using the template (Fig 31), trace the design onto the tissue paper.

2 Transfer the design onto the fabric (see Basic Techniques, page 13). Ensure that the centre lines align. When tacking, use a contrasting colour to your embroidery threads.

3 Attach the fabric to the frame (see Basic Techniques, page 14). Following the tacked lines carefully, stitch the outlines of the vine leaves and tendrils in backstitch with one thickness of Perlé. Rather than remove all the

(*Enlarge this template by 143%*)

Fig 31

tacking thread once you have completed your stitching, you may prefer to remove it a little at a time as you work.

4 Now stitch the trellis using the dark grey Coton à broder thread. Take care with the overlap of the sections and the position of the tendrils.

5 Work the blackwork stitches with the stranded cotton, using the stitch key to guide you. You may need to work some compensation or partial stitches (see Basic Techniques, page 19).

6 Check for mistakes and loose ends and remove from the frame. If

necessary, clean any soiled areas of the work then press (see Finishing Techniques, page 83).

7 This design requires a complicated mount and is quite difficult to stretch, therefore I suggest you ask a professional framer to do it. If you plan to use the frame for a mirror, you will not require glass to protect your piece of work.

8 If you wish, ignore the instructions to cut the fabric into a frame given above and, instead, embroider the centre of the work, adding your name and the date. Alternatively, simply elaborate the main design further.

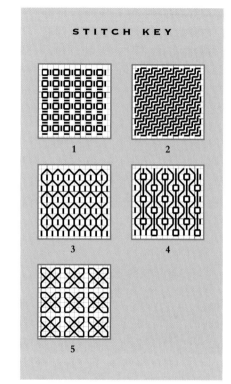

STITCH KEY

1 2 3 4 5

COLOUR KEY

	DMC Coton à broder	DMC Perlé	DMC Stranded	Size	Amount	Strands for backstitch	Strands for blackwork
	413			16	1 skein	1 thickness	
		310		8	1 ball	1 thickness	
			310		2 skeins		1

NB: use backstitch throughout and work it over two threads of the fabric.

HERB CUPBOARD

Familiar garden flowers and herbs are key motifs in English blackwork. They give the door of this herb cupboard a lovely, fresh look. Once you have mastered the design, you may wish to re-work a particular element as a smaller design, perhaps for a greetings card. Alternatively, why not work some of the plant designs individually and have them framed for your home?

SKILL LEVEL 3

DESIGN SIZE

10⁷⁄₁₆ X 13¾IN (264 X 350MM)

MATERIALS

Cream, 22 count Zweigart Oslo (264), 15 x 18in (380 x 459mm)

Sheet of good quality white tissue paper, 15 x 18in (380 x 459mm)

Size 26 tapestry needle

Tacking cotton in two contrasting colours (I've used black and red)

Hand-held frame, 12 x 18in (300 x 459mm)

Mahogany storage box, 16½ x 13in (430 x 330mm)

Threads as listed in the colour key

(Enlarge this template by 149%)

Fig 32

WORKING THE DESIGN

1 Trace the design onto the tissue paper using the black and red colouring pens where specified on the template (Fig 32).

2 Transfer the design onto the fabric using the same two colours of tacking cotton (see Basic Techniques, page 13). Try to ensure that the centre of the lines align.

3 Attach the fabric to the frame (see Basic Techniques, page 14). Following the tacked lines carefully, backstitch the outline of the shapes. This fabric has a fairly open weave, so take care to control the tension in your stitches to avoid creating holes. You can either remove the tacking thread once your stitching, is complete or remove it gradually as you work.

4 Next work the blackwork patterns within the red tacked shapes, using the stitch key to guide you. You may find it necessary to work some compensation or partial stitches (see Basic Techniques, page 19).

5 Check for any mistakes and loose ends. Ensure that you have removed all of the tacking thread and then remove the work from the frame. If necessary, clean your work, then press gently (see Finishing Techniques, page 83).

6 If you wish, you may stretch your work (see Finishing Techniques, page 83). Gently but firmly wrap your work around the board supplied with the cupboard, placing a sheet of acid-free paper between. Finally, insert the finished work into the front of your herb cupboard.

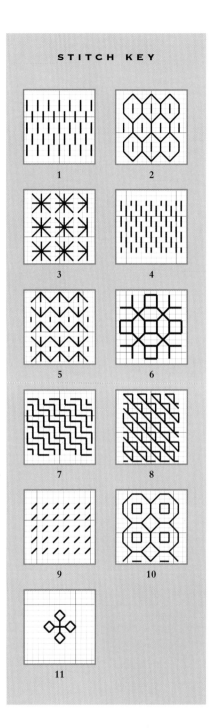

STITCH KEY

1 2 3 4 5 6 7 8 9 10 11

COLOUR KEY

	DMC Stranded	Amount	Strands for backstitch	Strands for blackwork
■■■	938	3 skeins	2	1

NB: for the outline, work each backstitch over one block of the fabric. For the patterns, each square on the blackwork chart equals 2 x 2 blocks.

CHAPTER TWO

CONTEMPORARY

BLACKWORK I

The designs in this chapter depart from the traditional

blackwork style because they are formed by full and

partial stitches and do not make use of a conventional

outline. I use tree forms to demonstrate this technique,

interpreting them in different ways: as a formal

design of regular tree shapes for the cushion,

a stylized design for the Christmas cards and

a naturalistic design for the Japanese landscape.

CHRISTMAS CARDS

These Christmas trees are worked in traditional festive colours and decked with strings of beads and silver or gold stars. Displayed in a complementary card mount, they make very special greetings cards for friends and family. You might like to extend the theme and work a row of them along the length of a runner to decorate your Christmas table.

SKILL LEVEL 1

DESIGN SIZE

3½ X 5IN (89 X 127MM)

STITCH COUNT

49 X 70

MATERIALS

White, 28 count Jobelan,
6 x 8in (152 x 203mm)

Christmas Green, 28 count Jobelan,
6 x 8in (152x 203mm)

Size 26 tapestry needle

Beading needle

Scarlet red beads

Gold and silver linen-embossed
card mounts

Threads as listed in the colour key

WORKING THE DESIGN

1 Find the centre of the fabric by folding it into four and mark it with a pin. Find the centre of the charted area by counting the squares and pencil a cross.

2 Working from the centre of the fabric outwards, stitch the rows of blackwork. Once you have completed this, add the stars.

3 Using a co-ordinating thread, stitch the beads in place. To secure the beads, darn through the back of the embroidery stitches between them.

4 Check for mistakes and loose ends. If necessary, clean your work and gently press (see Finishing Techniques, page 83).

5 Trim the fabric to fit the card mount and, ensuring that the tree is centred within the frame, affix with double-sided adhesive.

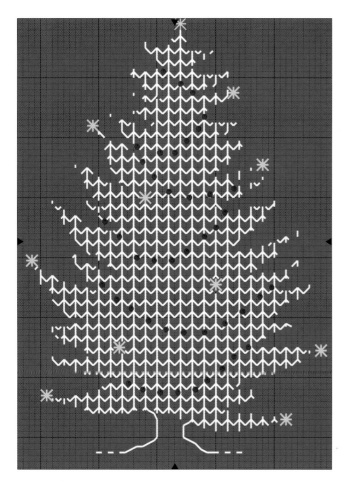
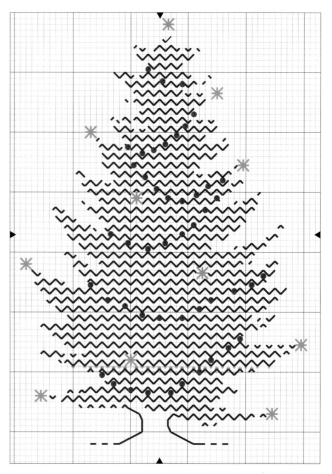

COLOUR KEY

	DMC Stranded	DMC Metallic	Amount	Strands for backstitch	Strands for blackwork	Strands for stars
	895		1 skein	2	1	
		Gold/Or	1 skein			1
	5200		1 skein	2	1	
		Silver/Argent	1 skein			1

NB. use backstitch or double running stitch throughout. Each square on the chart represents 2 x 2 threads of the fabric.

WINTER TREE CUSHION

This design is worked on a sage green background which co-ordinates nicely with the neat border of wintry trees. Dark green tassels at each corner of the cushion add further interest. The tree motif can be used elsewhere in your home – on placemats and napkins at the dining table or on pillowcases and curtains in the bedroom. If you wish, co-ordinate the colour scheme of the piece with your own decor for an entirely different look.

SKILL LEVEL 2
DESIGN SIZE
14⁵⁄₁₆ X 14⁵⁄₁₆IN (363 X 363MM)
STITCH COUNT
200 X 200

MATERIALS

Sage green, 14 count Zweigart Aida,
18 x 18in (459 x 459mm)

Plain furnishing fabric in
co-ordinating colour, 18 x 18in
(459 x 459mm)

Size 24 tapestry needle

Hand-held rectangular frame,
12 x 18in (300 x 459mm)

4 x cotton tassels

Threads as listed in the colour key

WORKING THE DESIGN

1 To centre the design on the fabric, fold it in half and tack a row of stitches along the fold. Fold in half again the other way and repeat.

2 Attach the fabric to your frame (see Basic Techniques, page 14).

3 To find the position of the inner line of the design, count 71 blocks outwards from the centre and begin stitching at this point. Count the squares to achieve a perfect square.

4 Next work the outer line which forms the tree trunks, then the blackwork trees.

5 Once you have completed the embroidery, check for mistakes and loose ends. Remove the work from its frame and press gently (see Finishing Techniques, page 83).

6 Tack a square measuring 17 x 17in (431 x 431mm) around the outside of the embroidered area, ensuring that the centre point of this square matches exactly that of the worked area. This marks the edge of the finished cushion and acts as a stitching guide.

7 You are now ready to make up the cushion (see Finishing Techniques, page 86).

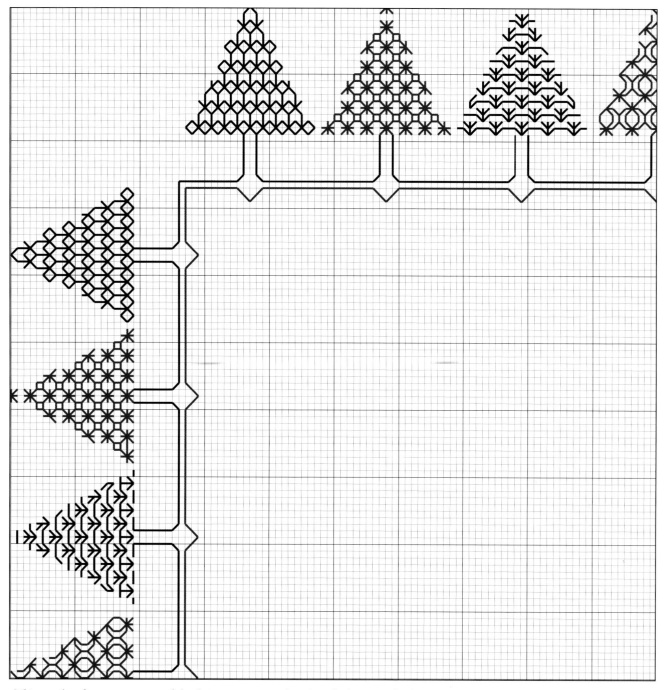

(This template forms one quarter of the design. Repeat template three further times for the complete cushion.)

COLOUR KEY

	DMC Stranded	Amount	Strands for blackwork	Strands for tree trunks & inner rectangle
▬	221	1 skein	1	2
▬	500	2 skeins	1	2

NB: each block of fabric is represented by one square on the chart.

JAPANESE LANDSCAPE PANEL

With this blackwork design, I have adapted the key natural elements of Japanese landscape art — a group of trees, a small island, hills in the distance — to create something different. As a result, I hope this project demonstrates the ways in which you might also develop traditional blackwork patterns in an innovative way.

SKILL LEVEL 3

DESIGN SIZE

13 X 7½IN (330 X 191MM)

STITCH COUNT

182 X 105

MATERIALS

Cream, 14 count Zweigart Aida,
18 x 13in (459 x 330mm)

Size 24 tapestry needle and
size 26 tapestry needle

Hand-held rectangular frame,
18 x 12in (459 x 300mm)

Tacking cotton

Threads as listed in the colour key

WORKING THE DESIGN

1 Fold the fabric in half and tack along the fold. Fold in half again and repeat. Mark the centre of the chart with a pencilled cross.

2 Mount the fabric on the frame (see Basic Techniques, page 14).

3 Following the colour key, work outwards from the centre of the design. Use a size 24 needle for cross-stitch and backstitch and a size 26 for pattern darning and blackwork.

4 Check for mistakes and loose ends.

5 Remove the fabric from the frame. If necessary, clean any soiled marks then gently press (see Finishing Techniques, page 83).

6 You may wish to stretch and mount your work by yourself (see Finishing Techniques, page 83). Alternatively, ask a professional framer to stretch, mount and frame it for you.

COLOUR KEY

	DMC Stranded	Amount	Strands for cross-stitch	Strands for backstitch	Strands for pattern darning	Strands for blackwork
	310	1 skein	2	2		1
	318	1 skein			1	1
	414	1 skein			1	1
	415	1 skein				1
	535	1 skein				1
	3799	1 skein		2		1

NB: the different greys in this design are represented on the chart by other colours to avoid confusion.

CHAPTER THREE

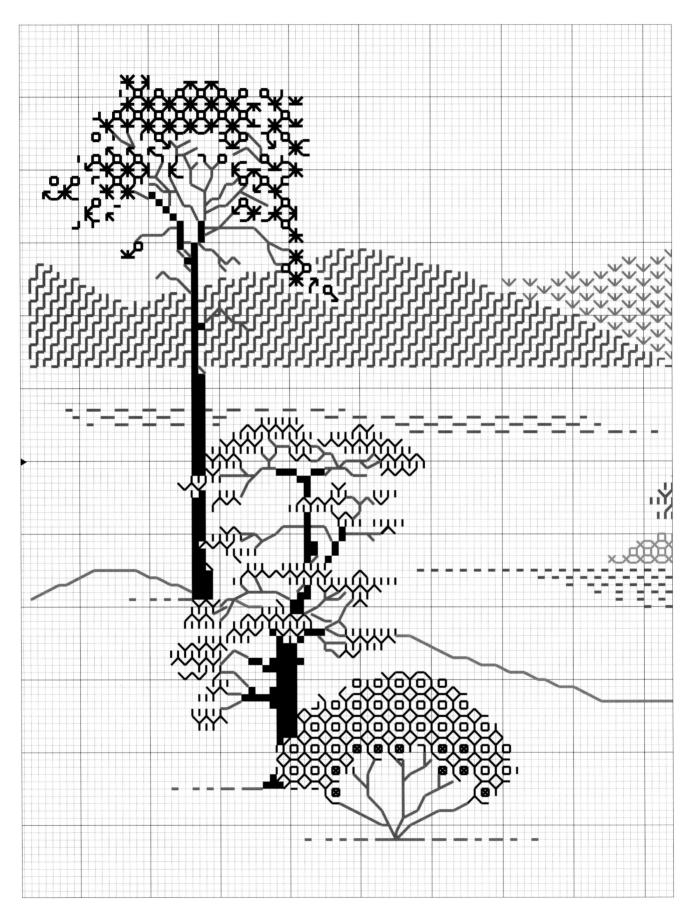

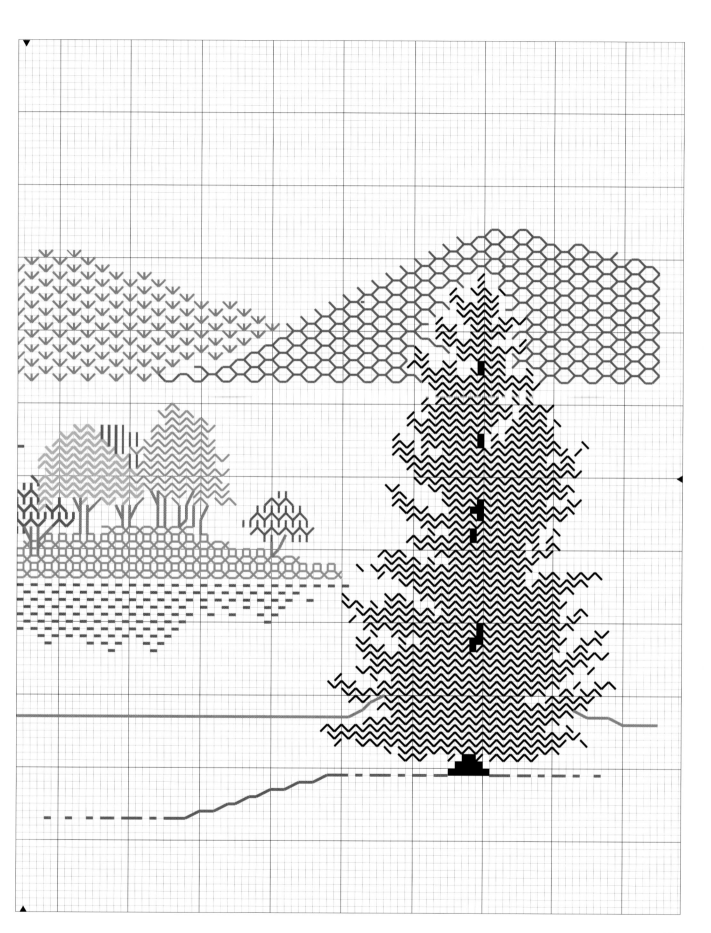

CONTEMPORARY

BLACKWORK II

In the last chapter I explored ways in which blackwork

is transformed by the addition of a new technique.

In this chapter I incorporate backstitch and couching

patterns into the blackwork designs to add complexity

to the pieces. Although these projects may appear

to be more complicated, the technique is very simple.

I hope that you enjoy tackling them!

AUTUMN LEAVES HAND TOWEL

This pretty hand towel is enriched by the use of backstitch to create veins and stems for the leaves. I have worked the design in shades of orange and brown on a cream background, but you can easily adapt the colours to your own decor, or extend the theme by creating a different colour scheme for each of the seasons.

SKILL LEVEL 1

DESIGN SIZE

18 X 2½IN (457 X 64MM)

MATERIALS

Cream, 16 count blockweave border
hand towel, 19 x 40in
(483 x 1014mm)

Size 26 tapestry needle

Sheet of good quality white
tissue paper the same size as
the towel panel

Tacking cotton in a
contrasting colour

Threads as listed in the colour key

WORKING THE DESIGN

1 Using the template (Fig 33), trace the design onto the tissue paper.

2 Ensuring that it lies straight on the weave, transfer the design onto the towel (see Basic Techniques, page 14).

3 Making use of compensation or partial stitches (see Basic Techniques, page 19), work the blackwork patterns. Follow the colour key and stitch key to guide you.

4 Stitch the veins and stems and, as you work, carefully remove the tacking.

5 Check the work for mistakes and loose ends. Ensure that all ends are securely darned on the back.

6 If necessary, clean your work and press gently (see Finishing Techniques, page 83).

STITCH KEY

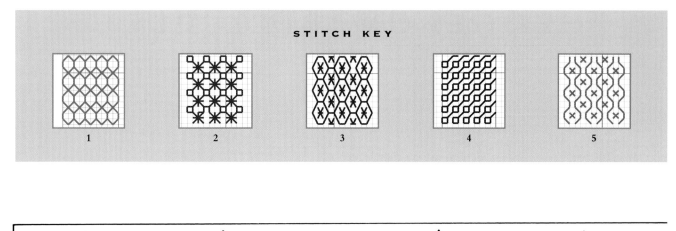

1   2   3   4   5

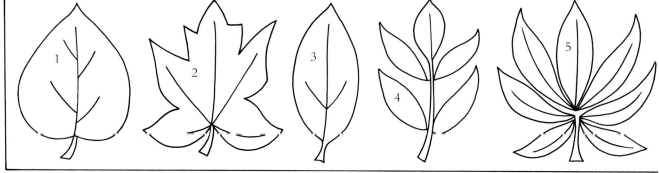

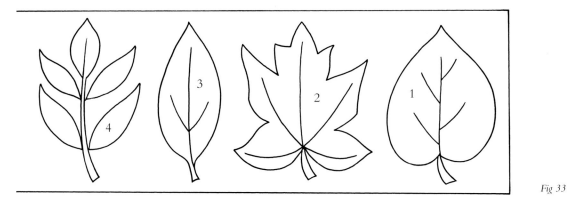

Fig 33

(Enlarge this template by 149% and join left- and right-hand sides together.)

COLOUR KEY

	DMC Stranded	Amount	Strands for blackwork	Strands for backstitch
	435	1 skein	1	
	610	1 skein	1	
	400	1 skein	1	
	3371	1 skein		1

HEDGEROW BELL PULL

*This design is based on the popular leaf, berry and hip motifs used
in traditional blackwork embroidery. It is worked on an evenweave band and,
with the addition of a narrow length of ribbon and a two-tone tassel,
makes a very eye-catching project for the home.*

SKILL LEVEL 2

DESIGN SIZE

15¼IN X 2¼IN (387 X 57MM)

SIZE OF COMPLETED BELL PULL

17 X 3¼IN (430 X 80MM)

MATERIALS

White, 28 count Zweigart evenweave
band (7347/1),
20in (503mm)

Forest green, 3mm double-face satin
ribbon, 1yd (1m)

Size 26 tapestry needle

Wooden bell pull ends,
5in (126mm)

A two-tone cotton tassel

1 sheet of good quality white tissue
paper the same size as the band

Tacking cotton

WORKING THE DESIGN

1 Using the template (Fig 34), trace
the design onto the tissue paper.
2 Ensuring that the design is centred,
transfer the design onto the panel
(see Basic Techniques, page 14),
placing the first unit 2in (50mm)
from the top of the band.
3 Working compensation or partial
stitches (see Basic Techniques, page
19) and following the colour key and
stitch key, complete all of the
blackwork patterns.
4 Backstitch the veins, stems and
tendrils and finish the top of each
hip with a fly stitch. Remove the
tacking as you work or once you
have completed the embroidery.
5 Before you go any further with the
bell pull, check the work for mistakes
and loose ends.

6 Thread the ribbon through the
slots in the edge of the band,
trimming it to the same length.
7 Turn over the top edge of the band
1in (25mm) and sew a hem just deep
enough for the wooden crossbar to fit
through. (You may need to trim the
crossbar to fit.) Insert it into the hem.
8 Following Fig 35, and ensuring
that the point at the bottom of the
band is centred, turn under the edge
from both sides once, 1in (25mm)
away from the embroidery. Cut ½in
(12mm) beyond these folds,
trimming away any surplus fabric.
Fold under a ¼in (6mm) hem. Stitch
into place, mitring the point and
catching in the ribbon as you do so.
9 Sew the tassel at the point of the
panel, and give the work a final press
(see Finishing Techniques, page 87).

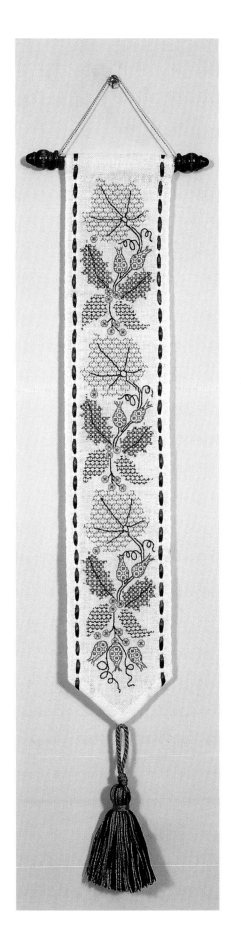

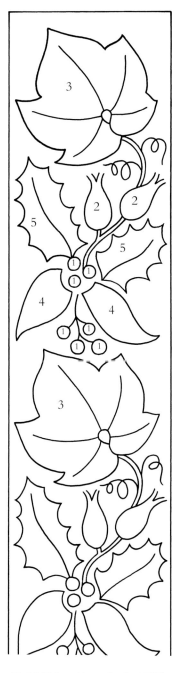

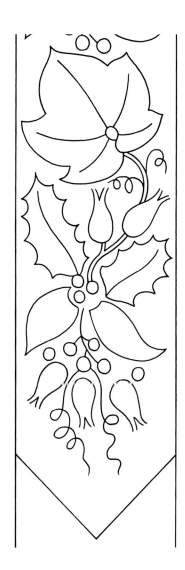

Fig 34 (Enlarge this template by 142%)

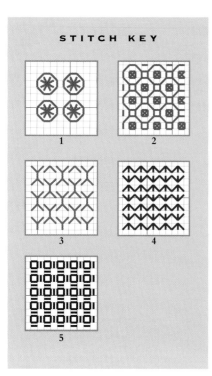

STITCH KEY

1

2

3

4

5

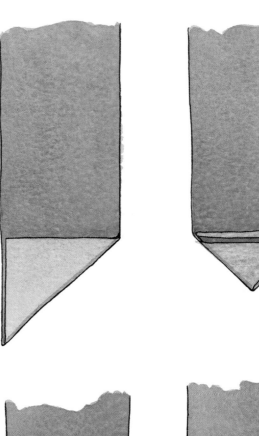

Figs 35a, b, c and d

COLOUR KEY

	DMC Stranded	Amount	Strands for blackwork	Strands for backstitch	Strands for flystitch
	720	1 skein	1	2	2
	502	1 skein	1		
	500	1 skein	1	2	
	699	1 skein	1	2	

SHEEP WALL PANEL

*This design uses only one blackwork stitch, worked in different tones of colour
to build up the forms of the sheep. The sheep are so charming that I have only hinted
at a background in order to emphasize them. They make an attractive motif
and you may wish to use them elsewhere – perhaps on a cushion cover or
as a border to curtains for a child's room.*

SKILL LEVEL 3

DESIGN SIZE

13¾ X 10IN (324 X 253MM)

MATERIALS

Ivory, 28 count Zweigart Jubilee (101),
22 x 18in (564 x 457mm)

Sizes 20 and 26 tapestry needles

Size 10 crewel needle

1 sheet good quality white tissue paper

Tacking cotton

Hand-held rectangular frame,
12 x 24in (300 x 600mm)

COLOUR KEY

	DMC Stranded	DMC Coton à broder	Cotton Perlé	Size	Amount
▬	310				1 skein
▬	413				2 skeins
▬	414				1 skein
▬	3022				1 skein
▬		310		25	2 skeins
▬			310	3	1 skein

WORKING THE DESIGN

1 Using the template (Fig 36), trace the design onto the tissue paper.

2 Ensuring that the design is centred, transfer the design onto the fabric (see Basic Techniques, page 13).

3 You are ready to work the sheep. Begin with the body of the front sitting sheep using the Coton à broder thread and working the basic form of blackwork stitch (see 1 in the stitch key). Where necessary, also work compensation or partial stitches (see Basic Techniques, page 19).

4 Carefully following the tacked areas, further work the next two stages of the stitches in the appropriate sections (see 2 and 3 in the stitch key).

5 To work the face and horns, use the size 20 tapestry needle and Perlé cotton, threading the couching thread through to the back of the fabric. Switch to the crewel needle and, using a single strand of stranded cotton, stitch down the couching thread.

6 For the shaded areas of the sheep's horns, backstitch, using a single strand of stranded cotton. For the sheep's face, nose and ears, use two strands of stranded cotton and cross-stitch.

7 Carefully following the threads key, work the remaining sheep in the same way.

8 For the background, darn small areas using a single strand of stranded cotton, working over the threads in the following pattern: 3-1-3-1-3 (see 4 in the stitch key).

9 Check for mistakes and loose ends and carefully remove the tacking.

10 Gently press your work (see Finishing Techniques, page 83).

11 You may wish to stretch the embroidery yourself (see Finishing Techniques, page 83). Alternatively, ask a professional framer to stretch, mount and frame it under glass for you.

Fig 36

(Enlarge this template by 190%)

THREAD KEY

	Front sheep (sitting)	Front sheep (standing)	Centre sheep (left)	Centre sheep	Rear sheep
Body	1 strand Coton à broder, 310	1 strand Coton à broder, 310	1 strand stranded cotton, 413	1 strand stranded cotton, 413	1 strand stranded cotton, 414
Outline on horns	1 strand Cotton Perlé, 310, couching stitch	1 strand Cotton Perlé, 310, couching stitch			
Shading on horns	1 strand stranded cotton, 310, backstitch	1 strand stranded cotton, 310, backstitch			
Face, ears, nose	2 strands stranded cotton, 310, cross-stitch	2 strands stranded cotton, 310, cross-stitch	2 strands stranded cotton, 310, cross-stitch	2 strands stranded cotton of both 310 & 413, cross-stitch	
Legs		2 strands stranded cotton, 310, cross-stitch			
Shading on legs		1 strand stranded cotton, 310, backstitch	2 strands stranded cotton, 413, cross-stitch	2 strand stranded cotton, 413, cross-stitch	
Outline on top of head		1 strand Coton à broder, 310, backstitch			
Outline, back leg			1 strand Coton à broder, 310, couching stitch		
Shading below head				1 strand stranded cotton, 310	
Head					2 strands stranded cotton, 413, cross-stitch

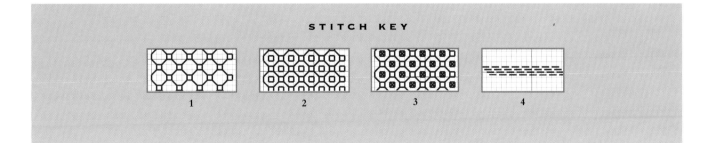

STITCH KEY

1   2   3   4

CHAPTER FOUR

NEGATIVE IMAGES

Blackwork patterns can sometimes form a

background to an outlined shape to great effect and

this is called making a negative image. The

designs in this chapter offer the embroiderer three

different interpretations of this technique:

a geometric design on a cushion, a Charles Rennie

Mackintosh-style rose design on a place mat and

napkin, and a wall panel of a Tudor manor.

ISLAMIC CUSHION

Geometric and arabesque patterns found in Islamic and Spanish architecture have a strong historical connection to English blackwork and continue to influence contemporary embroidery. This design is inspired by the beautiful fretwork designs such as those featured in the Alhambra in Granada. The star motif, intricate patterns and highlights of colour combine to form a striking whole which is adaptable to other items in your home.

SKILL LEVEL 1

DESIGN SIZE

9⁷⁄₁₆ X 9⁷⁄₁₆IN (239 X 239MM)

CUSHION SIZE 17 X 17IN (431 X 431MM)

STITCH COUNT

132 X 132

MATERIALS

Navy, 14 count Zweigart Aida (589),
18 x 18 in (459 x 459mm)

Furnishing fabric in a co-ordinating
colour, 18 x 18in (459 x 459mm)

Size 24 and 26 tapestry needles

Hand-held rectangular frame,
12 x 24in (300 x 600mm)

Tacking cotton

Threads as listed in the key

WORKING THE DESIGN

1 To centre the design on the fabric, fold it in half and tack along its length. Fold in half again the other way and repeat.

2 Mount the fabric onto the frame (see Basic Techniques, page 14).

3 Following the chart carefully, work outwards from the centre of the fabric. First stitch all the outlines in backstitch using a single thickness of Coton à broder and then fill in the blackwork patterns.

4 Once you have completed the embroidery, check for mistakes and loose ends and remove the tacking.

5 Remove from the frame and press (see Finishing Techniques, page 83).

6 Tack a square measuring 17 x 17in (431 x 431mm) around the outside edge of the embroidery, ensuring that the centre of this square matches exactly the centre of the embroidery. This square marks the shape of the finished cushion and acts as a stitching guide.

7 Having completed the above, you are now ready to make up your piece of embroidery as a cushion (see Finishing Techniques, page 86).

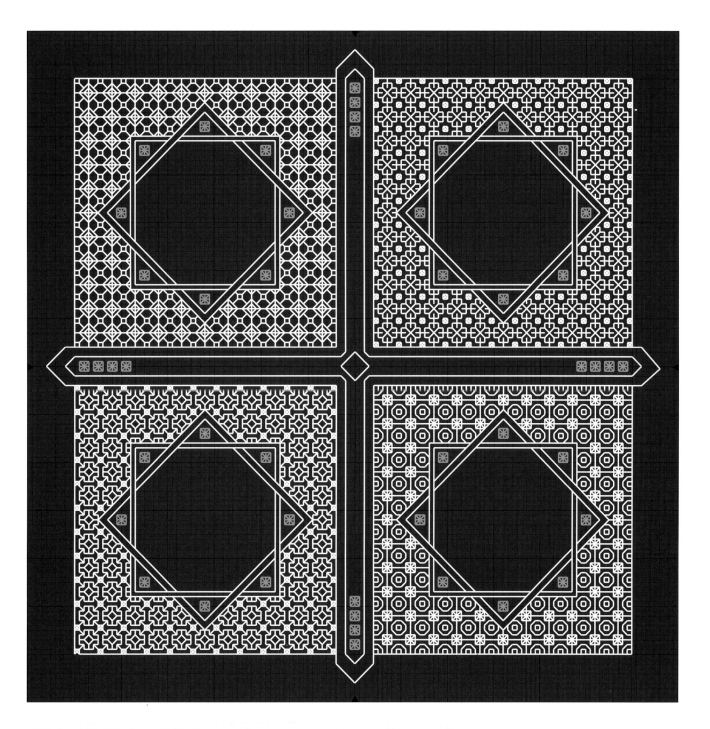

COLOUR KEY

	DMC Coton à broder	DMC Stranded	Size	Amount	Strands for backstitch	Strands for blackwork
	Blanc		16	1 skein	1	1
		Blanc		2 skeins		
		995		1 skein		1

NB: each square on the chart represents one block of the fabric.

MACKINTOSH TABLE LINEN

Charles Rennie Mackintosh was an exponent of the Art Nouveau movement and his distinctive style remains popular today. The design for this set of co-ordinating place mat and napkin is based upon Mackintosh's classic rose motif. The colour scheme of pink, grey and white is also typical of Mackintosh although, if you prefer, you might like to experiment with alternative colours to create something different.

SKILL LEVEL 2

DESIGN SIZE

PLACE MAT 1½ X 6⅞IN

(44 X 176MM)

NAPKIN 1⅝ X 1⅝IN (42 X 42MM)

STITCH COUNT

PLACE MAT 24 X 97

NAPKIN 23 X 23

MATERIALS

White place mat and napkin
with Aida panels

Size 20 and 26 tapestry needles

Threads as listed in the key

WORKING THE DESIGN

1 The design for this place mat is small enough for you to work in the hand. Begin the design by stitching the four large squares in dark grey stranded cotton at the base of the design and, once completed, work your way up until you reach the rose motif and the leaves.

2 Couch the rose and leaves (see Basic Techniques, page 17) using the size 20 tapestry needle for the couching thread.

3 Your table linen will need to be frequently washed, so it is advisable to stitch your thread ends as securely as you can.

4 Fill in the blackwork pattern to the background, paying attention to the tension in your stitches: a tight stitch will distort the fabric.

5 Once you have completed the embroidery, check for mistakes and loose ends. Gently press (see Finishing Techniques, page 83).

6 Now work the napkin. You will, by now, be familiar with the design and it is simply a matter of translating one element to a smaller area.

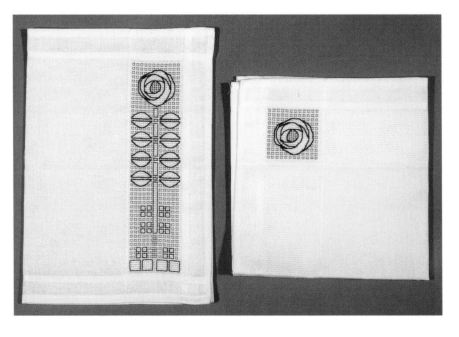

COLOUR KEY

DMC Stranded	Amount
317	1 skein
961	1 skein
3799	1 skein

NB: each square on the chart represents one block of the Aida panel.

THREAD KEY

Outline

1 thickness (6 strands) stranded cotton, 3799, stitched down with 1 strand

Dark Grey blocks

2 strands stranded cotton 3799, backstitch

Blackwork background pattern

1 strand stranded cotton, 317

Pink infill

2 strands, stranded cotton, 961

TUDOR MANOR WALL PANEL

This design is based upon a timbered Tudor building, beautiful examples of which still exist. Apart from a few simple patterns which emulate the decoration characteristic of these buildings, I have not over-worked them to provide contrast with the more complex, freely stitched blackwork patterns which form the landscape.

SKILL LEVEL 3

DESIGN SIZE

12$\frac{7}{16}$ X 6$\frac{7}{8}$IN (314 X 176MM)

STITCH COUNT

173 X 97

MATERIALS

White, 28 count Zweigart Brittney,
15 x 11in (380 x 279mm)

Size 26 tapestry needle

Hand-held rectangular frame,
12 x 15in (300 x 376mm)

Threads as listed in the key

WORKING THE DESIGN

1 Find the centre of the fabric by folding into four and marking it with a pin. To find the centre of the chart, count the squares and pencil a cross.

2 Mount the fabric onto the frame (see Basic Techniques, page 14). As you work, ensure that the fabric is pulled completely taut.

3 Working outwards from the centre, begin to stitch the design. Complete the building, using 1 thickness of Coton à broder, before any other section of the piece – it will act as a stitching guide for the patterns on the building and the blackwork patterns for the landscape. If necessary, work some compensation or partial stitches (see Basic Techniques, page 19).

4 Once you have completed this, check for mistakes and loose ends. If necessary, clean any soiled areas and press your work (see Finishing techniques, page 83).

5 You may wish to stretch and mount your work (see Finishing Techniques, page 83). Alternatively, if you are not comfortable with the task, ask a professional framer to stretch, mount and frame it under glass for you.

COLOUR KEY

	DMC Stranded	DMC Coton à broder	Size	Amount	Strands for blackwork	Strands for backstitch	Strands for pattern darning
		310	25	1 skein		1 thickness	
	355			1 skein	1		
	926			1 skein	1		
	832			1 skein	1		
	830			1 skcin	1		
	937			1 skein	1		1
	935			1 skein	1		
	3816			1 skein	1		
	991			1 skein	1		

NB: One square on the chart represents 2 x 2 threads of the fabric.

CHAPTER FIVE

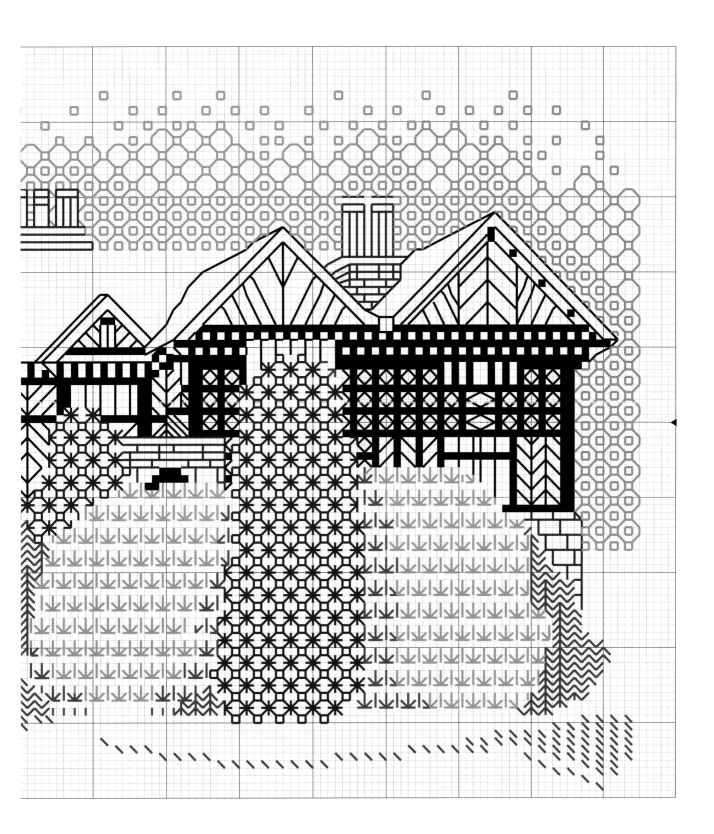

EXPERIMENTING
WITH COLOUR

In this chapter I use coloured fabrics and space-dyed

threads to enhance our work. I think you will

agree that they really lift the designs.

I am inspired by the mythic creatures and symbols

found in Celtic folklore and these projects offer the

perfect opportunity to experiment with both colour

and pattern in a contemporary way.

CELTIC KNOT LAVENDER BAGS

The celtic knot motif used in this design is a true classic. I have worked the design in four different, but complementary, natural colours and have also used different tones of the same colour to give the design a strong sense of form. This design would adapt well to other items in your home – perhaps on a cushion cover, or as a motif on a plain shirt or blouse.

SKILL LEVEL 1

DESIGN SIZE

3 X 3IN (76 X 76MM)

STITCH COUNT 42 X 42

MATERIALS

Light blue, forget-me-not blue, wood violet and blue wing,
28 count Jobelan,
two pieces of each, 5 x 7in
(126 x 175mm)

Size 26 tapestry needle

Blue mist, jade, light orchid and aqua 3mm double-face satin ribbon,
1yd (1m)

Dried lavender

Threads as listed in the key

WORKING THE DESIGN

1 Fold one of the two pieces of identical fabric in half along its length. Measure a point 2½in (64mm) from one end and mark with a pin. This gives you the position for the centre of the knot symbol. Following the chart, count outwards until you reach the outline of the design where you can begin to stitch.

2 Backstitch along the outline of the knot symbol.

3 Fill in the light and dark pattern sections. You may need to work compensation or partial stitches (see Basic Techniques, page 19).

4 Check for any mistakes and loose ends. If necessary, clean your work then gently press (see Finishing Techniques, page 83).

5 Now make up the lavender bag. Place the two pieces of fabric together with your embroidery facing in and stitch a ¼in (6mm) seam along one long side of the bag. Open out and turn a small hem along the top edge of the bag and stitch in place.

6 With right sides facing again, stitch the remaining long side and bottom.

7 Turn out once more and fill with dried lavender. Tie the neck with co-ordinating ribbon.

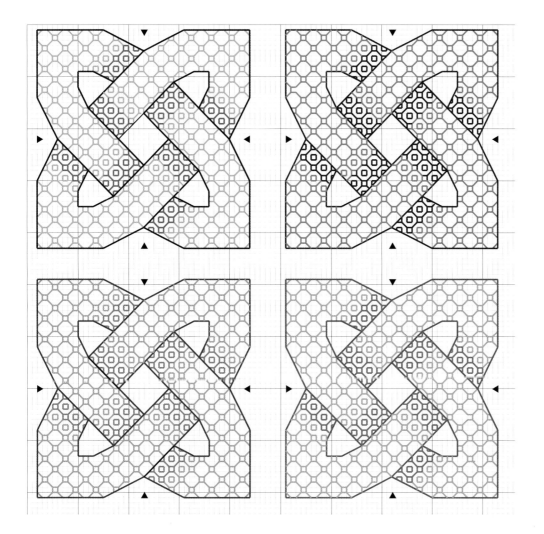

COLOUR KEY

	DMC Stranded	Strands for backstitch (outline)	Strands for shadow	Strands for backstitch (pattern)	Amount
	796	2			1 skein
	798		1		1 skein
	799			1	1 skein
	550	2	1		1 skein
	208			1	1 skein
	3812	2			1 skein
	958		1		1 skein
	959			1	1 skein
	924	2			1 skein
	3768		1		1 skein
	747			1	1 skein

NB: one square on the chart represents 2 x 2 threads of the fabric.

CELTIC HOUND CURTAIN TIE-BACK

The design on this striking tie-back features two hounds whose bodies are intertwined. The hound is a common feature of Celtic myth, representing hunting, healing and protection and can be seen in many examples of surviving Celtic manuscripts. The central section of each hound is worked in a space-dyed thread using a simple blackwork pattern and tiny areas of gold thread to highlight their eyes. These curious creatures would look stunning worked onto the lid of a wooden box or a cushion cover, perhaps with a border of gold metallic thread.

SKILL LEVEL 2

DESIGN SIZE

4 X 29IN (102 X 735MM)

COMPLETE TIE-BACK

5 X 33IN (127 X 837MM)

STITCH COUNT (ONE UNIT)

131 X 56

MATERIALS

Oatmeal 14 count Zweigart Yorkshire
Aida (54), 6 x 35in (152 x 890mm)

Co-ordinating cotton furnishing fabric,
6 x 35in (152 x 890mm)

Pelform stiffening, 4⅝ x 33in
(117 x 837mm)

Size 24 tapestry needle

Hand-held rectangular frame,
6 x 12in (150 x 300mm)

Two small brass rings

Threads as listed in the key

WORKING THE DESIGN

1 Mount the fabric onto the frame (see Basic Techniques, page 14).

2 Beginning 3in (76mm) from one end, work the hounds in cross-stitch, ensuring that they are centred on the fabric. Following the stitch key, and paying attention to the alteration in direction of stitches in the middle section of the hounds (see detail, over), work the bodies.

3 Work three repeats in total, leaving four complete rows of blocks between repeats.

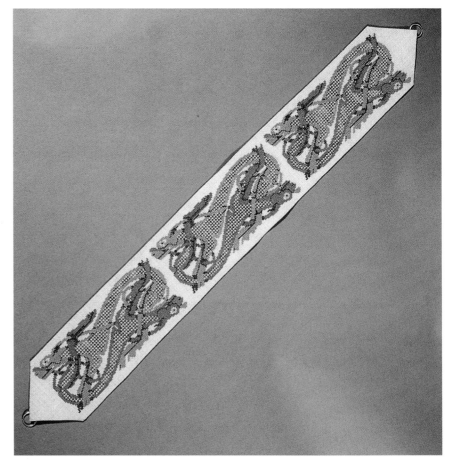

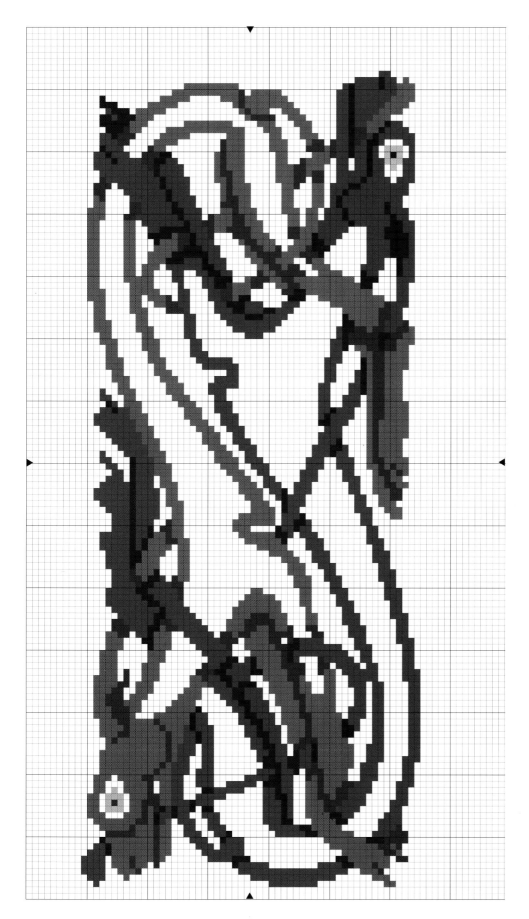

(Enlarge this template by 160%)

4 Use the metallic thread to work the eyes of the hounds.

5 Check for any mistakes and loose ends, then remove from the frame.

6 If necessary, clean any marks and then press your work (see Finishing Techniques, page 83).

7 Mitre the ends of the Pelform stiffening and check its length against that of the tie-back. It should project a good 2in (51mm) beyond each end of the embroidery.

8 Lay the embroidery face down on a clean surface and, ensuring that it is centred, place the Pelform stiffening on top. Peel off a section of backing paper, position the point and align the strip with the fabric weave.

9 Continue to peel off the backing and position it a little at a time until you reach the other end. Press into place. Trim the surplus fabric to ½in (12mm) around each of the points.

10 Remove the backing from the top side of the Pelform and turn the surplus fabric onto the adhesive surface, mitring the corners where it is necessary.

11 Place the lining fabric face down and centre the stiffened tie-back on top of it. Press into place. Trim the surplus fabric to ½in (12mm). Turn under this small hem and slip stitch the two pieces of fabric together.

12 Sew a small brass ring onto each end of the reverse side of the tie-back so that you can hang it neatly around your curtain – you can now mount it into position.

STITCH KEY

1

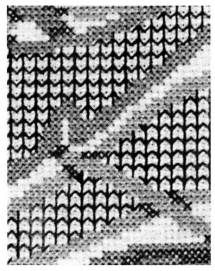

COLOUR KEY

	DMC Stranded	DMC Metallic Floss	Caron Wildflowers	Amount	Strands for blackwork	Strands for cross stitch	Strands for the eyes
	701			3 skeins		2	
	996			3 skeins		2	
	699			2 skeins		2	
	824			2 skeins		2	
		Gold/Or		1 skein			2
			Royal Jewels	1 skein	1		

NB: one square on the chart represents one block of the fabric and one cross stitch.

CELTIC KNOT TRAY

◆◆
◆◆

Inspired by the symmetrical planting of traditional Tudor knot gardens, I have worked this design so that a band of blackwork forms a path between two rows of interlacing knots. I have borrowed from the colours of the herb garden — sage green, lavender blue and allium pink — to fill in between the knot symbols and stitched beads to add sparkle. It would be equally satisfying to reproduce this design as a footrest, or, by selecting one knot only, to work a pretty top to your pincushion.

SKILL LEVEL 3

DESIGN SIZE

13¾ X 9½IN (350 X 240MM)

MATERIALS

Twilight blue, 28 count Fabric
Flair Minster linen, 20 x 16in
(510 x 400mm)

Size 20 and 26 tapestry needles

Size 10 crewel or beading needle

1 packet mauve beads

Hand-held rectangular frame,
12 x 18in (300 x 459mm)

Tacking cotton in
contrasting colours

Good quality white tissue paper

Tray blank

Threads as listed in the key

WORKING THE DESIGN

1 Using the template (Fig 37), trace the design onto the tissue paper.

2 Ensuring that the design is centred, transfer it onto the fabric (see

Basic Techniques, page 13).

3 Following the stitch key, first work the central pathway, aligning the straight edge of the chart with the two end knot units and working the

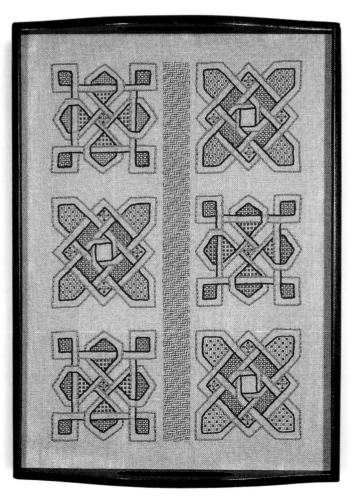

(Enlarge this template by 160%)

Fig 37

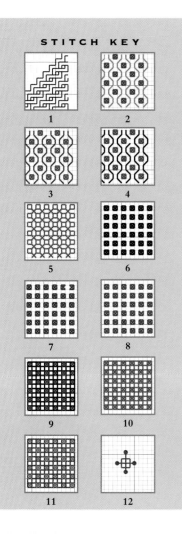

STITCH KEY

1 2 3 4 5 6 7 8 9 10 11 12

pattern centrally over the centre tacked row. Continue with the pattern until you reach a row level with the last two knot motifs. Finish the pattern on this line to match the beginning of the pathway.

4 Following the tacked lines carefully, couch the knot shapes, using the darker thread for the inner line of each band and the lighter for the outer line.

5 Use the size 20 tapestry needle to take the couching thread through to the back of the fabric, and stitch in place with one strand of matching stranded cotton. Secure in place on the back with one or two small stitches, ensuring that they are not visible on the front of the work.

6 Fill in between the outlines with the patterns, using compensation or partial stitches where necessary. Check the chart, stitch and colour key to guide which pattern and colour thread and how many strands of each to use.

7 Using a co-ordinating thread, add the mauve beads to the small motifs.

8 Once completed, check for any mistakes and loose ends and remove any tacking which may still be visible on the work. (The tacking used to outline the knot motifs will now be disguised by the couching, so you needn't remove it.)

9 Remove the embroidery from the frame and press gently (see Finishing Techniques, page 83).

10 You may wish to stretch the embroidery yourself (see Finishing Techniques, page 83), using the board supplied with the tray.

11 To insert the stretched embroidery into the tray, follow the instructions supplied by the manufacturer, but omit the oval cut-out. If you are using a different tray, perhaps one you have picked up or already own, follow the instructions given for mounting a piece of work (see Finishing Techniques, page 83).

COLOUR KEY

	DMC Stranded	DMC Soft Embroidery	Amount	Strands for blackwork	Stitch key references	Strands for couching	Strands for stitching down
	3768		1 skein	1	1		1
		2926	1 skein			1 thickness	
		2924	1 skein			1 thickness	
	553		1 skein	1	2/11		
	3350		1 skein	1	3/10		
	924		1 skein	1			1
	327		1 skein	1	2/8/11		
	315		1 skein	1	3/7/10		
	469		1 skein	2	12		
	333		1 skein	1	4/9		
	3740		1 skein	2	5		
	791		1 skein	1	4/6/9		

NB: one square on the chart represents 2 x 2 threads of the fabric.

CHAPTER SIX

USING ACCESSORIES

In this final project chapter I use accessories —

charms, beads and metal threads — to really lift the

designs. Don't be afraid to be bold with them;

there are many different kinds of accessory to choose

from and not only do they add interest to your work,

they are an immense amount of fun.

HONEY BEES LIDDED JARS

This design is inspired by the most industrious of workers, the bee. Indeed, the bee and the embroiderer have much in common – both produce striking designs to create something functional yet beautiful. To honour this connection, I have added metal thread to a formal pattern of honeycomb and clover to decorate the larger of the two porcelain bowls and added a pretty gilt bee to complete the effect. You may wish to extend the theme and work the spray of clover onto a handkerchief or as a greetings card, perhaps substituting the bee with a little gilt butterfly.

SKILL LEVEL 1

DESIGN SIZE (SMALL BOWL)

1¼ X 1¼IN (30 X 30MM)

STITCH COUNT

34 X 33

MATERIALS

White, 28 count Zweigart Jubilee,
6 x 6in (153 x 153mm)

Lightweight iron-on Vilene,
4 x 4in (102 x 102mm)

Embroidery hoop,
4in (100mm) in diameter

Size 26 tapestry needle

Pack of charms

Soft green porcelain lidded jar

Threads as listed in the key

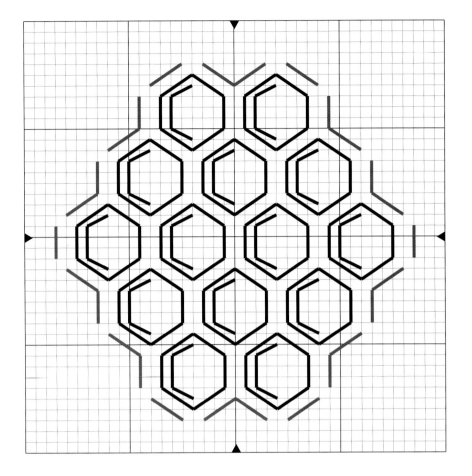

WORKING THE DESIGN

1 To find the centre of the fabric, fold it into four and mark it with a pin. To find the centre of the charted area, count the squares on the design. Pencil the centre of the chart with a cross.

2 For this design it is best to use an embroidery hoop to work the embroidery. Insert the fabric into the hoop, ensuring that the weave is straight in both directions and that the fabric is completely taut.

3 Working from the centre of the chart, begin to work the design using backstitch or double running stitch.

4 Once you have completed the embroidery, check for mistakes and loose threads then gently press (see Finishing Techniques, page 83).

5 Centre the iron-on Vilene over the back of the embroidered area of the fabric and gently press with the iron.

6 Sew the bee charm onto your embroidery.

7 Following the instructions supplied with the jar, discard the acetate and trim the embroidery to fit the lid.

COLOUR KEY

	DMC Stranded	Amount	Strands for backstitch
▬▬▬	310	1 skein	1
▬▬▬	317	1 skein	1

NB: each square on the chart represents 2 x 2 threads of the fabric.

SKILL LEVEL 2

DESIGN SIZE (LARGE BOWL)

3¼ X 3⅛IN (81 X 79MM)

STITCH COUNT

86 X 87

MATERIALS

White, 28 count Zweigart Jubilee,
8 x 8in (204 x 204mm)

Light-weight iron-on Vilene,
6 x 6in (153 x 153mm)

Embroidery hoop,
6in (150mm) in diameter

Size 26 tapestry needle

Pack of charms

Soft green porcelain lidded jar

Threads as listed in the key

WORKING THE DESIGN

1 To find the centre of the fabric, fold it into four and mark it with a pin. To find the centre of the charted area, count the squares on the design. Pencil the centre of the chart with a cross.

2 Insert the fabric into the embroidery hoop, ensuring that the weave is straight in both directions.

3 Count outwards from the centre of the chart to the nearest stitch and begin to work the design, using backstitch or double running stitch.

4 Once you have completed the embroidery, check for mistakes and loose threads then gently press (see Finishing Techniques, page 83).

5 Centre the iron-on Vilene over the back of the embroidered area and gently iron.

6 Sew on the bee charm.

7 Following the instructions supplied with the bowl, discard the acetate and trim the embroidery to fit the lid.

COLOUR KEY

	DMC Stranded	Amount	Strands for backstitch (honeycomb)	Strands for backstitch (clover outline)	Strands for backstitch (clover flowers)	Strands for markings on leaves
▬	310	1 skein	1	2	1	
▬	317	1 skein				1
▬	Or/Gold	1 skein	1			

NB: each square on the chart represents 2 x 2 threads of the fabric.

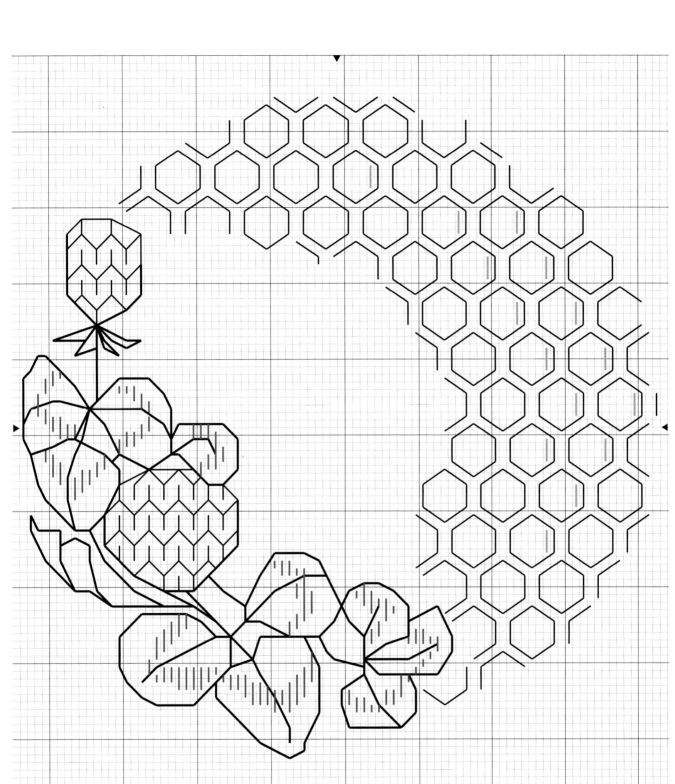

BOX LID

This design is based upon a floor tile. It uses a variety of attractive elements — metallic threads and eye-catching beads — which will inspire you to incorporate accessories into your own designs. If you wish, substitute the rich Victorian red colour scheme for your own — summery pastel shades with patterns worked in a contrasting tone would give your work a contemporary look.

SKILL LEVEL 2

DESIGN SIZE

4½ X 4½IN (115 X 115MM)

STITCH COUNT

66 X 66

MATERIALS

Victorian Red, 28 count Zweigart Brittney, 8 x 8in (204 x 204mm)

Hand-held rectangular frame, 6 x 12in (150 x 300mm)

Size 26 tapestry needle

Beading needle

Wooden box blank with a 5 x 5in (128 x 128mm) cut-out in the lid

Piece of stiff card, 4½ x 4½in (125 x 125mm)

Black, grey and antique silver beads

Threads as listed in the key

COLOUR KEY

	DMC Stranded	DMC Metallic	Amount
	5200		1 skein
		Silver/Argent	1 skein
	3799		1 skein
	318		1 skein
	310		1 skein

NB: each square on the chart represents 2 x 2 threads of the fabric.

WORKING THE DESIGN

1 To find the centre of the fabric, fold it into four and mark it with a pin. To find the centre of the charted area, count the squares on the design. Pencil the centre of the chart with a cross.

2 Mount the fabric in the frame, ensuring that it has an even tension.

3 Working outwards from the centre of the chart, stitch the central motif (but do not add the beads).

4 Using the appropriate stitches and threads (see charts), work the outlines of the oblong shapes.

5 Once you have completed this, use the outlines to guide your stitches for the borders and motifs.

6 Consulting the chart and using the co-ordinating dark grey, pale grey and black threads, attach the beads.

7 Check your work for loose ends and remove from the frame. Press gently (see Finishing Techniques, page 83).

8 You can now mount your work into the top of the wooden box (see Finishing Techniques, page 83).

THREAD KEY

Central square and four projecting arms	Cross-stitch in outer border	Motifs and pattern borders	Inner edge of larger rectangle	All other lines
1 strand metallic thread, chain stitch	1 strand metallic thread	1 strand stranded cotton, 5200, backstitch	2 strands stranded cotton, 5200, whipped backstitch	2 strands stranded cotton, 5200, backstitch

CHESSBOARD

For this design, repeating patterns have a functional as well as decorative use. I have worked a variety of patterns in herringbone stitch in an unusual and, I hope, striking interpretation of the chessboard design. Once completed, I am certain it will provide your friends and family with hours of pleasure! If, however, you do not have a chess-player among your acquaintances, this design would work equally well as a cushion cover, perhaps with gold and silver tassels.

SKILL LEVEL 3

DESIGN SIZE

15¾ X 15¾IN (400 X 400MM)

STITCH COUNT

220 X 220

MATERIALS

19½ x 19½in (495 x 495mm) Zweigart
14 count Aida (323)

Hand-held rectangular frame,
12 x 24in (300 x 600mm)

Size 26 tapestry needle

Tacking cotton

Threads as listed in the key

WORKING THE DESIGN

1 Fold the fabric in half and tack a line of stitches along this fold. At right angles to this first row, fold and tack a row of stitches in the other direction.

2 Consulting the chessboard chart, continue to tack further rows on each side of the centre fold, leaving 28 blocks between each until you have ninelines in each direction.

3 Mount the fabric onto the frame (see Basic Techniques, page 14). Roll the fabric on so that the first row of squares is visible and begin to stitch at this point.

4 Working in backstitch with two strands of black stranded thread, stitch a square twenty-four blocks in size in the centre of each tacked square.

5 Consulting the chart, fill in the first row of squares with the appropriate blackwork patterns and borders. Work each row until the design is complete.

6 Now work the lines of herringbone stitch. Metallic thread has a tendency to slip out of the eye of the needle while you work. To help prevent this, rather than work with two strands of metallic thread, use a longer single strand of metallic thread, doubled.

7 Once you have completed the embroidery, remove all tacking stitches, check your work for loose ends and remove from the frame then press gently (see Finishing Techniques, page 83).

8 You may wish to stretch the embroidery and mount it onto the board yourself (see Finishing Techniques, page 83). Alternatively, take it to a professional framer and ask to have it stretched, mounted and framed under glass. Please note, however, that the framer should allow clearance so that the glass is not in contact with the embroidery.

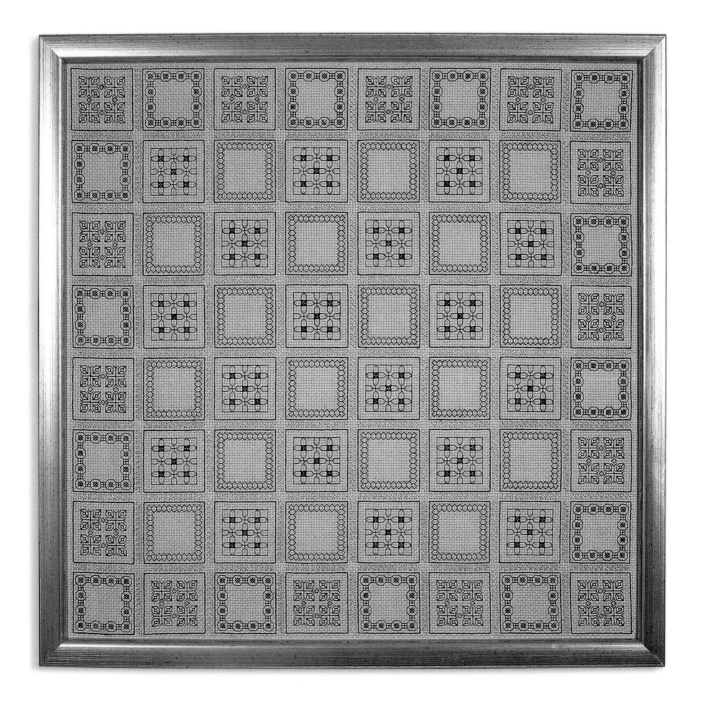

(For a complete chessboard, repeat this template as a mirror image. If necessary; please refer to the photograph, page 79.)

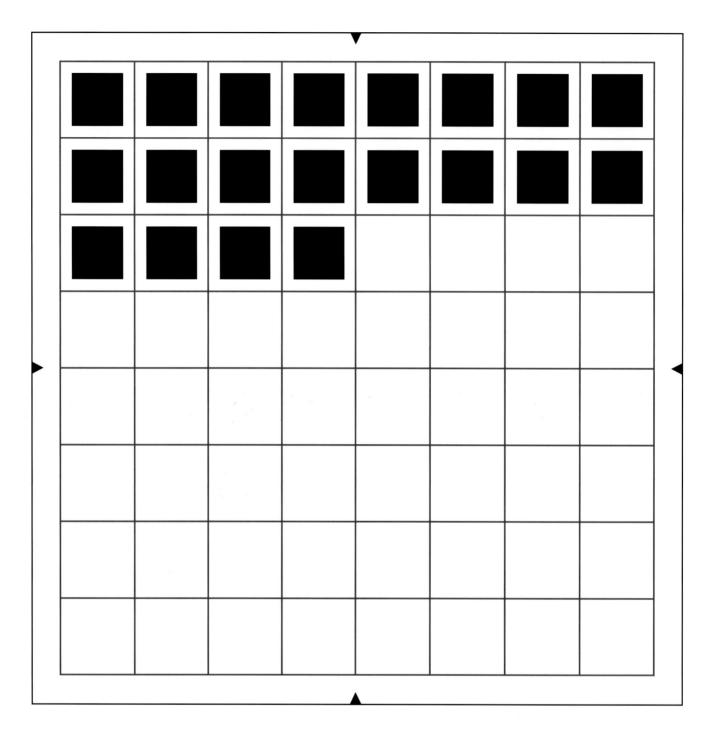

COLOUR KEY

	DMC Stranded	DMC Metallic	Amount	Strands for outline of squares	Strands for blackwork	Strands for herringbone
▬	310		4 skeins	2	1	
		Gold/Or	1 skein			2
		Silver/Argent	1 skein			2

NB: each square on the chart represents one block of the fabric.

FINISHING TECHNIQUES

By the time you reach this stage you will have spent many hours of painstaking work on a project and, hopefully, have gained an enormous amount of satisfaction from completing a beautiful piece of work. You must now finish off your item properly, clean it if necessary and decide how you wish to display it. It is worth spending a little time on this final stage so that you end up with something of which you can be truly proud.

CLEANING

If you have worked your embroidery in a frame it should only require a light press. However, if your work has been soiled, immerse it in a solution of lukewarm water and either a mild detergent or traditional soap flakes and swirl it gently in the suds. Never scrub your embroidery, it will damage the stitches and distort the material. Your threads should be colourfast, but if you experience some running (red is sometimes unstable), rinse in cold water until it stops. Rinse thoroughly several times to remove all traces of soap. Remove your embroidery from the water and squeeze (not wring) excess water out very gently before rolling the embroidery in a towel and squeezing again. Press your embroidery while still damp.

PRESSING

To press, place the embroidery face down on a soft, folded towel and place a fine, dry cloth over it. Apply the iron gently, lifting and pressing small areas and gradually working over the whole piece. Do not press too hard or drag the iron across the work as this will flatten and distort your stitches. Repeat as often as necessary until it is smooth and completely dry. To press dry embroidery, use a damp cloth instead of a dry one. A steam iron will not be necessary for this task.

MOUNTING AND FRAMING

Unless you are an adept framer, it is advisable to have your work framed by a reputable, professional framer. However, there is no reason why you should not mount and stretch your work yourself. Indeed, it is a useful and satisfying skill to learn for future projects.

MATERIALS

Acid-free mount board (the density should relate to the size of your embroidery: larger pieces will require thicker board. Alternatively, use Cormount, a dense polystyrene foam sandwiched between two paper skins)

Craft knife

Metal ruler

Cutting mat

Strong thread for lacing

Round-headed pins

First, decide whether you want to use wadding underneath your fabric to raise it slightly from the surface of the mount board. Then decide how much of your finished work you would like to display and tack a provisional 'frame' onto the fabric. Mark out

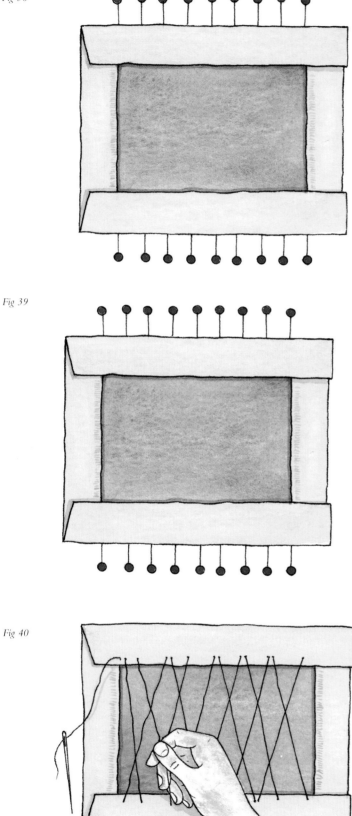

Fig 38

Fig 39

Fig 40

on the board an area slightly smaller than this measurement. Cut the board carefully, making several shallow cuts rather than a single deep one. Position the embroidery face down on a clean surface and, keeping within the tacked line, place the board on top. Beginning at the mid-point of the top edge, insert pins through the fabric into the edge of the board to hold it in place. Ensuring that the fabric is taut, gently pull the fabric over the bottom edge and continue to pin. Repeat on the left- and right-hand sides. Use the tacked line to ensure that the grain of the fabric lies true on the board (Fig 38). Using a long length of strong thread and working from the centre, lace from side to side across the back, working stitches every inch (25mm) or so (Fig 39). Leave a length free at the end. Complete the second half, then remove the pins on these two sides. Starting from the centre, pull each thread in turn to tighten the lacing and fasten off securely at both ends (Fig 40). Lace the two remaining sides together in the same way (Fig 41). It is not necessary to remove the original tacked line as it should be disguised by the frame. Your work is ready to frame.

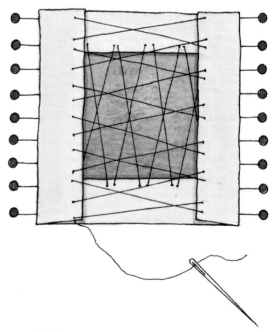

Fig 41

MOUNTING INTO CARDS

Card mounts are the ideal way to display smaller pieces of blackwork and to send as greetings to friends and family. The cards for mounting embroidery are readily available and easy to use, with a fold-over section to hold the fabric neatly in position. The following instructions for mounting blackwork onto a card applies to all sizes.

MATERIALS

Card mount

Glue or double-sided adhesive tape

Iron-on non-woven interfacing

(for larger pieces)

Small embroidered motifs need only pressing before mounting, but for larger pieces it is advisable to support the back of your work with iron-on non-woven interfacing. Place the embroidery face up on a clean surface. Check that the embroidery fits comfortably within the frame of the card mount by placing it opened out on top of it. You may need to trim the edges of the fabric if they project beyond the central area of the card. Remove the card mount, turn it over and run a line of glue or double-sided tape about ¼in (6mm) around the window, on the wrong side (Fig 42). Turn the card over and, with the front facing you, lower it onto the embroidery. Press into place. Place the card face down again and run a line of glue or double-sided tape around the four edges of the left-hand section. Fold this over onto the back of the embroidery, covering it completely and press firmly (Fig 43).

Fig 42

Fig 43

MAKING UP A CUSHION

The cushion projects in this book can be made using the following tried-and-tested method.

MATERIALS

Cotton fabric cut to the same size as
your embroidered piece
Machine thread
Dressmaker's pins
Cushion pad very slightly larger than your
projected cover (for a nice, plump cushion)

Tack a square the same size as your finished cushion, ensuring that the centre of the square matches exactly the centre of the embroidered design. With right sides facing, pin the front and back together. Machine or backstitch along three sides of the cushion, plus an extra 3in (76mm) at either end of the final side. Mitre the corners as shown and trim the seam allowance to ½in (12mm) (Fig 44). Turn the cushion cover right side out and insert the pad. Fold under and crease the seam allowance along the edges of the opening to give a stitching guide. Using ladder stitch, sew up the opening. Ensure that the small stitches are at right angles to the seam. Pull gently on the thread as you work to bring the two edges together.

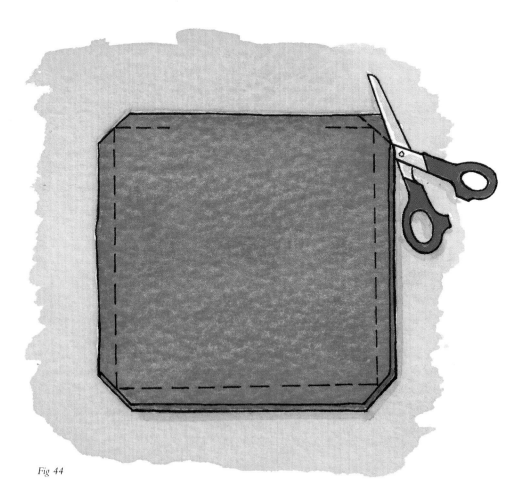

Fig 44

MAKING A BASIC TASSEL

Cut a piece of cardboard the same length as the desired length of the skirt of your tassel. Decide how full you would like the skirt to be and wind as many threads of stranded cotton (or other suitable thread) as you desire around it. Loop a matching thread between the wound threads and the edge of your piece of cardboard, pull up tightly and tie with a secure knot (Fig 45). At the bottom of the skirt, carefully cut the wound threads and remove the cardboard. Using matching thread, make a loop (Fig 46). Bind the threads as tightly as possible around the waist of the skirt and knot the ends (Fig 47). Trim the bottom of the tassel so that the threads are all the same length – and you have a beautiful tassel to complement your embroidery.

Fig 45

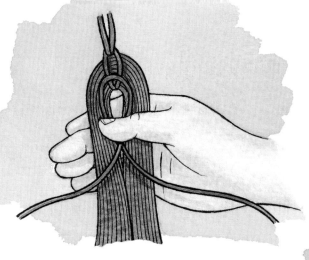

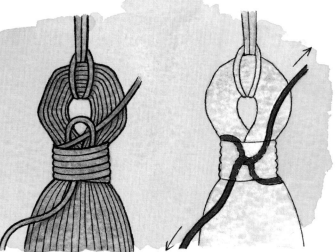

Fig 46

Fig 47

GETTING STARTED WITH YOUR OWN DESIGNS

If you have followed the projects in this book chapter by chapter you will, by now, be more than proficient in a number of techniques and have experimented with colour and accessories to enhance your work. Following an experienced embroiderer's designs is a good way to learn technique, but I hope that you have, like me, developed an enthusiasm for blackwork and be keen to try out your own designs.

MATERIALS
Sheets of black paper
Sheets of pale-coloured paper
(cream, pale grey or white)
Black and white crayon or
charcoal and white chalk
An old newspaper
Small pieces of card, 6 x 4in
(150 x 100mm)
Pair of scissors
Paste or glue
Graph paper
Tissue paper

MAKING MARKS ON PAPER

Getting started with your own designs can seem more than a little daunting at first. I have seen many students with a blank sheet of paper in front of them and an equally blank expression! There is nothing quite so discouraging as a virgin page, as any writer will testify. But do not despair. The best way to approach embroiderer's block is to force yourself to make some marks on paper – however provisional and dreadful they may be! Simply by putting pencil or charcoal to paper helps to break down your worries about getting started with a design. It is really a very liberating experience and it is amazing how quickly your confidence grows.

Before you begin, decide what medium you would like to work in. You do not have to use a hard pencil – I like to use crayon, charcoal or chalk which enable you to produce a looser, more textured mark.

Using first a black crayon on its side on a contrasting background colour, build up a series of geometric motifs. Now use the white crayon on a dark background and repeat. Overlap some of your marks to experiment with density of tone (Figs 48a & b). Now arrange the marks in a formal repeating pattern. There are many combinations which you can later develop, but only make additional marks if you feel it improves the overall design, not simply for its own sake.

There are other, equally helpful, methods for getting started on your design. Instead of using crayon, charcoal or chalk, cut regular shapes of different print densities out of the newspaper. Experiment with different combinations of patterns until you produce one that you like, then paste them down (Figs 49a & b). Or, why not use a stencil to build up a pattern? Take a piece of thin card, 4 x 6in (100 x 150mm), and fold it in half. Cut a simple leaf shape out of the fold and then open the card out. Using a crayon or piece of chalk, colour in the cut-out shape. Continue to do this until you form a simple repeating pattern which might be developed into a pattern for a project (Fig 50). You can use the same technique in reverse. Take the cut-out leaf shape and, using your crayon, colour the background around it. Continue to do this until you have a simple repeating pattern. If you feel they improve the design, add veins to the leaves, too (Fig 51). You now have two versions of the same motif: one black on white, the other white on black – an arrangement known as counterchange. Use both versions of the motif to make an alternating repeating pattern or border (Figs 52a & b).

Think about how to interpret the light and dense areas into stitched blackwork patterns. There are at least two techniques you might employ to achieve this. You can either work a light blackwork pattern and then work additional stitches into it to create the dense areas or you can work a blackwork pattern in a fine thread, substituting it for a thicker thread for the dense areas (Figs 53a & b). You might also use different shades of the same colour or lighter and darker colours to represent tonal qualities, for example white, grey and black. The thread count of your fabric will also influence the density of the patterns (see Materials and Equipment, page 8). A pattern worked on a 32 count evenweave linen, a tightly-woven fabric, will look very different if worked on an 11 count Aida, which has a larger scale

and produces a more open pattern (Figs 54a & b).

You have now experimented with various media to take practical steps towards understanding how to develop your ideas into designs using blackwork patterns. You must now translate these patterns into an accurate template for your design. Return to the first geometric motifs you produced. Using a soft pencil, transfer them onto graph paper, ensuring that the proportions remain consistent throughout (Figs

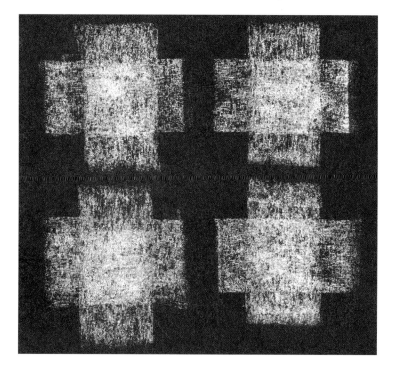

Figs 48a & b

Figs 49a & b

55a, b & c). As you plan your design onto the graph paper, it is essential to keep in mind that it will appear larger on the graph paper than on your chosen fabric, for example if the size of your motif is going to be 2 x 2in (50 x 50mm) and you plan to work it on 14 count Aida, it will translate as 28 x 28 squares on your chart.

Once you have finalized your design and mapped it onto graph paper, you must decide on the nature of your project – perhaps you would like to work it for a cushion cover or the lid of a box. This decision is crucial as you must consider the scale of your design in relation to the project. Equally, you must consider the fabric count and the thickness of threads. To help you decide on these interrelated factors, you might find it helpful to work small samples of stitches on off-cuts of different count fabrics to ensure the threads pass comfortably through the weave, before setting out your design. It is better to make adjustments to the thread count at this stage than on the finished piece.

You are now ready to set out the design onto the fabric – a procedure with which you will be very familiar by now! Fold your fabric in half and half again and tack a row of stitches along these centre

folds in a bold colour. If necessary, mount your fabric onto your frame. If your design has a centre motif, begin to stitch outwards from the centre. If not, you must carefully count to find your correct position. Once you have worked all areas of blackwork, you can sew any beads or charms you wish to use to decorate it, using co-ordinating threads. Ensure that any loose threads are neatly secured. Finish off your work by giving it a gentle press. This method works

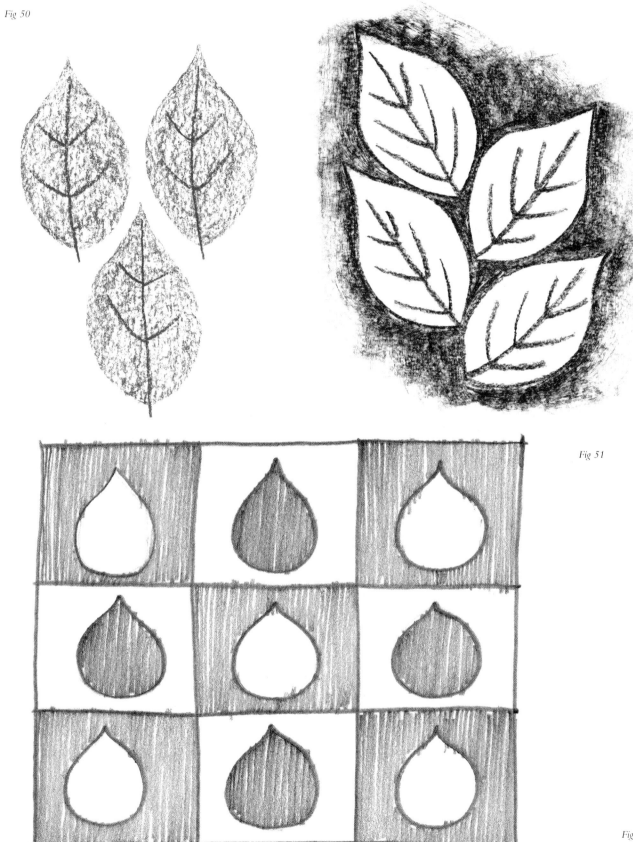

Fig 50

Fig 51

Fig 52a

Fig 52b

Figs 53a & b

Figs 54a & b

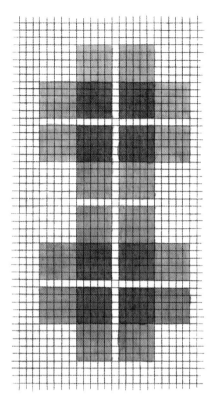

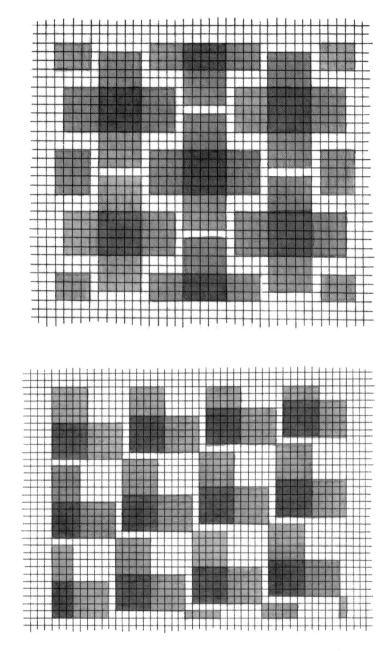

very well for geometric motifs, but you will need to approach your design differently if it is based on an irregular motif like the leaf you stencilled. You may wish to reduce or enlarge the motif. The simplest way to do this is to use a photocopier. However, if you do not have access to one, follow these straightforward instructions:

1 Draw a rectangle around the design. The rectangle should measure to the nearest inch or centimetre in both directions to aid planning the next stage (Fig 56).

2 Cut out the rectangle. Position it on top of a larger sheet of paper and line it up with the bottom left-hand corner.

3 Draw a diagonal line from the bottom left-hand corner of the sheet of paper containing your design through its top right-hand corner and across the larger sheet of paper.

4 Decide by how much you wish to enlarge the design. Produce an enlarged rectangle with the same proportion as the original by drawing first a vertical and then a horizontal line from your chosen point on the diagonal (Fig 57).

5 Take the smaller rectangle and, using a pencil, divide it into a grid (Fig 58).

6 Now take the enlarged rectangle and divide into

the same number of squares, which will be larger.

Figs 55a, b & c

7 Plot the position of your design onto the larger rectangle with a series of dots, matching each square on the small rectangle with its counterpart on the large one (Fig 59). Finally, join up the dots. This method can be used in reverse to reduce the size of your design.

8 Once you have enlarged or reduced your motif, transfer your design onto your fabric. The best way to transfer a non-geometric shape onto fabric is to trace the design onto tissue paper and tack along the traced lines. From here, proceed as before.

Fig 56

Fig 57

SEEKING INSPIRATION

Once you have mastered the techniques described so far, the next important task is to seek out inspiration around you for your designs. You really need not go far – there are numerous designs waiting to happen in your own garden. Take note of the shapes and patterns formed by plants and flowers and make sketches or take photographs and keep them safe in an 'ideas' scrapbook. When you go out, look more closely at the architecture of interesting buildings; churches, for example. You may not live near to somewhere quite as thrilling as the Alhambra, but you will soon find all kinds of inspiring patterns and textures for your work. Another good source of inspiration is your local library or book shop. Leaf through books on art and design or, indeed, anything else – you are just as likely to find something of interest in a book on travel or wildlife. Sometimes a good design source will fall into your lap – postcards from friends and family, an item of clothing, a piece of fabric in a shop or a picture in a magazine.

Visual references are very important, but your own ideas and motivations are equally so. Perhaps you have a passion outside of embroidery which inspires you, for example bird-watching or the theatre? If you have a hobby, draw on it for inspiration and utilize whatever it offers for your designs.

Words are another good source of inspiration – do you have a favourite poem? Have you read a piece in a newspaper which provokes you? Are you moved by a particular song lyric?

It is also useful to think about colour. Pay attention to colours around you which work well together. Nature provides us with beautiful combinations, for example the changes in the seasons – forest green and holly berry red in winter or lemon yellow and lime green in spring; or the contrasts of landscape – a steely grey sky against a blue-green sea. As the project chapters demonstrate, blackwork needn't mean simply working black on white (although, as a historic combination, it is a great favourite). Before long, you will have a packed scrapbook of ideas from which to

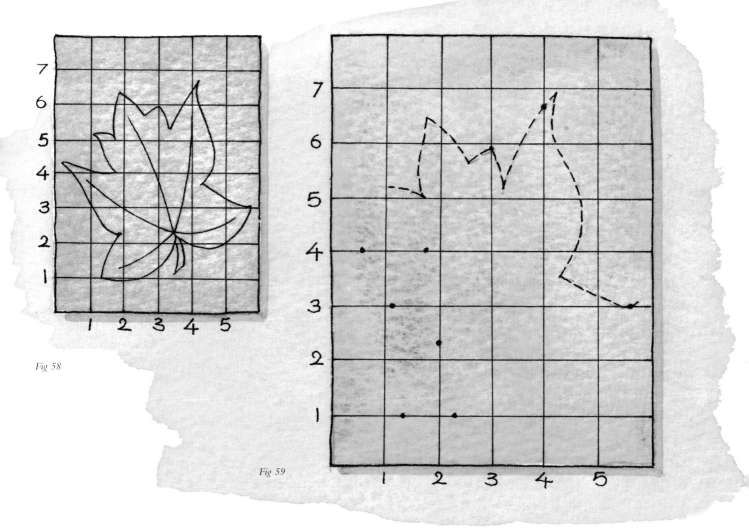

Fig 58

Fig 59

develop your designs – enough to keep you going for a dozen projects! Once you have a couple of clear ideas, the next step is to think about how to translate them into a design. Take time to think about examples of embroidery you have seen which you admire and the purpose and function of the project upon which you are embarking. You may wish to develop your ideas into abstract motifs like the Islamic cushion cover project, or work them into a more literal representation like the sheep wall panel project. You may wish to combine both, perhaps working a landscape as the focus of your piece and picking out a motif as a border.

A good way to think through these things is to create a storyboard which combines your photographs, sketches, notes and pattern designs. I include two examples of storyboard layouts to demonstrate what I mean (Figs 60 & 61). You will

also find two blank storyboards and a page for making notes to help you work out your own ideas.

As you can see, bringing all the elements of your ideas together enables you to see how your design might develop. In the knot garden storyboard, the layout of the formal gardens are suggestive of a myriad abstract patterns for you to elaborate into a design. In the sheep panel storyboard, the shapes and textures of the sheep are also very suggestive. Their three-dimensional nature also forces you to think about how to represent tonal qualities in your work. The world is now your oyster, as the saying goes! I have only two further pieces of advice for you before you go and create beautiful pieces of work. The first is: whatever you attempt, keep it small and simple – don't run before you can walk. The second is: if you do make mistakes, always put it down to experience.

Good luck and happy designing!

Fig 60. Sheep storyboard

Soay ram

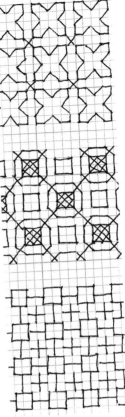

Small wall panel worked
in blackwork, using areas of
tonal patterns without outline.
Heads and horns worked in
cross-stitch and backstitch.

Fig 61. Knot garden storyboard

A repeating pattern which might translate into a cushion

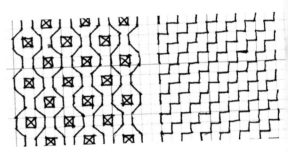

Knot unit could be repeated four times to fit a cushion, or one unit for small square tray. Area between tramlines worked in blackwork pattern – shaded area in slightly heavier thread than rest, to give overlap.

17th century knot garden designs

Border round edge of
rectangular tray

Details from two
knot gardens used
for repeat pattern
on tray

Area of blackwork
without outline

SOURCES OF INFORMATION
AND SUPPLIERS

❖❖
❖❖

MUSEUMS, HISTORIC HOUSES AND SOCIETIES

Many museums hold collections of blackwork embroidery in the United Kingdom and in North America. The items held in these collections are not simply beautiful examples of embroidery, but interesting records of our social history. Such things provide valuable general information and may inspire your own blackwork designs and further research – it can become addictive! If you want specific information about a piece it is best to write to the curator, stating exactly what you wish to know. If you want to view something it is advisable to telephone in advance for an appointment in case the item you want to see is not on public view.

United Kingdom

The Burrell Collection
Pollok Country Park
2060 Pollokshaws Road
Glasgow G43 1AT
Tel: 0141 649 7151

The Embroiderer's Guild
Apartment 41
Hampton Court Palace
Surrey KT8 9AU
Tel: 0181 943 1229

The Gallery of Costume
Platt Hall
Rusholme
Manchester M14 5LL
Tel: 0161 224 5217

Maidstone Museum and Art Gallery
St Faith's Street
Maidstone
Kent ME14 1LH
Tel: 01622 754497

The Middleton Collection
Castlegate Museum
51 Castlegate
Nottingham
Nottinghamshire NG1 6AF
Tel: 0115 915 3500/5555

Museum of London
London Wall
London EC2Y 5HN
Tel: 0171 600 3699

Parham Park
Pulborough
West Sussex RH20 4HS
Tel: 01903742021

Royal Museum
Chambers Street
Edinburgh EH1 1JF
Scotland
Tel: 0131 225 7534

The Royal School of Needlework
Apartment 21a
Hampton Court Palace
Surrey KT8 9AU
Tel: 0181 943 1432
(The School organizes day courses specializing in hand embroidery, including blackwork.)

Victoria and Albert Museum
Cromwell Road
South Kensington
London SW7 2RL
Tel: 0171-938 8500

Whitworth Art Gallery
University of Manchester
Oxford Road
Manchester M15 6ER
Tel: 0161 275 7450

United States of America and Canada

The Art Institute of Chicago
111 South Michigan Avenue
Chicago
Illinois 60603–6110
Tel: 312 443 3600

The Brooklyn Museum
200 Eastern Parkway
Brooklyn
New York City
New York 11238
Tel: 718 638 5000

Indianapolis Museum of Art
1200 West 38th Street
Indianapolis
Indiana 46208
Tel: 317 923 1331

The Metropolitan Museum of Art
1000 Fifth Avenue
5th Avenue at 82nd Street
New York City
New York 10028
Tel: 212 879 5500

The Museum of Fine Arts
465 Huntington Avenue
Boston
Massuchusetts 02115
Tel: 617 267 9300

National Museum of History and
Technology
Smithsonian Institute
14th Street and Constitution Avenue
Washington DC 20560
Tel: 202 357 2700

Royal Ontario Museum
100 Queens Park
Toronto
Ontario M5S 2C6
Tel: 416 586 5549

BOOKS

The brief list which follows includes
some titles which are currently out of
print and these are marked ★.
However, they may be found at your
local library or purchased from
second-hand book shops.

Arthur, Liz, *Embroidery 1600 – 1700
at the Burrell Collection,*
John Murray/Glasgow Museums,
Glasgow, 1995★

Barnett, Lesley, *Blackwork,* Search Press,
UK, 1996, ISBN 0 855 32806 1

Geddes, Elizabeth & McNeill, Moyra,
Blackwork Embroidery,
Dover Publications, UK, 1976,
ISBN 0 486 23245 X

Gostelow, Mary, *Blackwork,*
Dover Publications, UK, 1998,
ISBN 0 486 40178 2

Gray, Nicolette, *The History of Lettering,*
Phaidon, London, UK, 1986, ISBN 0
7148 2334 1

Hughes, Therle, *English Domestic
Needlework,* Lutterworth Press, London,
1961★

Jones, Owen, *Grammar of Ornament,*
Dover Publications, UK, 1988,
ISBN 0 486 25463 1

Liley, Alison, *The Craft of Embroidery,*
Mills and Boon Ltd, London, 1961★

MacAlpine, Joan, *The Shadow of the
Tower,* BBC Books, London, UK,
1971★

Nevinson, John L., *Catalogue of English
Domestic Embroidery,* H.M.S.O., London,
1938 (reprinted 1950)★

Thomas, Mary, *Dictionary of Embroidery
Stitches,* Hodder and Stoughton Ltd,
London, 1934 (reprinted 1956)★

SUPPLIERS

United Kingdom

DMC Creative World Ltd
Pullman Road
Wigston
Leicestershire LE18 2DY
(DMC threads, Zweigart fabrics)

Fabric Flair Ltd
Northlands Industrial Estate
Copheap Lane
Warminster
Wiltshire BA12 OB9
(Jobelan fabric, Minster linen, hand
towel, place mat and napkin, beads)

Framecraft
372/376 Summer Lane
Hockley
Birmingham B19 3Q
(bell pull ends, charms, tray and
lidded jars)

Glyn Owen
Afallon
Church Hill
Glyn Ceiriog
Llangollen LL20 7DN
(wooden box blank)

Macleod Craft Marketing
West Yonderton
Warlock Road
Bridge of Weir
Renfrewshire PA11 3SR
(Caron threads)

Market Square
28 Portway
Warminster
Wiltshire BA12 8QD
(herb cupboard blank)

Offray Ribbon
Ashbury
Co. Tipperary
Eire
(satin ribbon)

Willow Fabrics
95 Town Lane
Mobberley
Cheshire WA16 7HH
(Zweigart fabrics)

United States of America

The Caron Collection
67 Poland Street
Bridgeport CT 06605
(Caron threads)

C.M. Offray & Son Inc.
Route 24
Box 601
Chester NJ 07930-0601
(satin ribbons)

DMC Corp.
Port Kearny
Building 10
South Kearny NJ 07032
(DMC threads)

Joan Toggit Ltd
2 Riverside Drive
Somerset NJ 07032
(Zweigart fabrics)

Sudbery House
Colton Road
Box 895
Old Lyme CT 0637
(tray, lidded jars, charms,
bell pull ends)

Wichelt Imports Inc.
Route 1
Highway 35
Stoddart WI 54658
(Jobelan fabrics)

ABOUT THE AUTHOR

*Brenda Day was born in Warrington, Cheshire. She trained as an embroideress at
Bromley College of Art and then at Manchester College of Art.
After gaining her Art Teachers' Certificate in 1959 she spent several years
teaching children and adults alike until leaving to raise a family. This coincided with
a move to Wales where she continues to live.*

*In the intervening period she has won a number of awards for her design work while working
as co-partner in her husband's business. In 1988 she set up a successful embroidery kit
business aimed at the Welsh tourist market which produces designs inspired by art, wildlife,
and Celtic and Welsh themes. Brenda also works as a freelance designer for a variety of
companies, including some national magazines.*

INDEX

Blank storyboard

Blank storyboard

NOTES

NOTES

NOTES

TITLES AVAILABLE FROM

GMC Publications

BOOKS

Woodcarving

The Art of the Woodcarver	*GMC Publications*	Relief Carving in Wood: A Practical Introduction	*Chris Pye*
Beginning Woodcarving	*GMC Publications*	Understanding Woodcarving	*GMC Publications*
Carving Architectural Detail in Wood: The Classical Tradition		Understanding Woodcarving in the Round	*GMC Publications*
	Frederick Wilbur	Useful Techniques for Woodcarvers	*GMC Publications*
Carving Birds & Beasts	*GMC Publications*	Wildfowl Carving – Volume 1	*Jim Pearce*
Carving the Human Figure: Studies in Wood and Stone		Wildfowl Carving – Volume 2	*Jim Pearce*
	Dick Onians	Woodcarving: A Complete Course	*Ron Butterfield*
Carving Nature: Wildlife Studies in Wood	*Frank Fox-Wilson*	Woodcarving: A Foundation Course	*Zoë Gertner*
Carving Realistic Birds	*David Tippey*	Woodcarving for Beginners	*GMC Publications*
Decorative Woodcarving	*Jeremy Williams*	*Woodcarving* Tools & Equipment Test Reports	*GMC Publications*
Elements of Woodcarving	*Chris Pye*	Woodcarving Tools, Materials & Equipment	*Chris Pye*
Essential Woodcarving Techniques	*Dick Onians*	Making & Using Working Drawings for Realistic Model Animals	
Lettercarving in Wood: A Practical Course	*Chris Pye*		*Basil F. Fordham*
Power Tools for Woodcarving	*David Tippey*		

Woodturning

Adventures in Woodturning	*David Springett*	Turning Miniatures in Wood	*John Sainsbury*
Bert Marsh: Woodturner	*Bert Marsh*	Turning Pens and Pencils	*Kip Christensen & Rex Burningham*
Bowl Turning Techniques Masterclass	*Tony Boase*	Understanding Woodturning	*Ann & Bob Phillips*
Colouring Techniques for Woodturners	*Jan Sanders*	Useful Techniques for Woodturners	*GMC Publications*
Contemporary Turned Wood: New Perspectives in a Rich		Useful Woodturning Projects	*GMC Publications*
Tradition		Woodturning: Bowls, Platters, Hollow Forms, Vases,	
	Ray Leier, Jan Peters & Kevin Wallace	Vessels, Bottles, Flasks, Tankards, Plates	*GMC Publications*
The Craftsman Woodturner	*Peter Child*	Woodturning: A Foundation Course (New Edition)	*Keith Rowley*
Decorating Turned Wood: The Maker's Eye	*Liz & Michael O'Donnell*	Woodturning: A Fresh Approach	*Robert Chapman*
Decorative Techniques for Woodturners	*Hilary Bowen*	Woodturning: An Individual Approach	*Dave Regester*
Fun at the Lathe	*R.C. Bell*	Woodturning: A Source Book of Shapes	*John Hunnex*
Illustrated Woodturning Techniques	*John Hunnex*	Woodturning Jewellery	*Hilary Bowen*
Intermediate Woodturning Projects	*GMC Publications*	Woodturning Masterclass	*Tony Boase*
Keith Rowley's Woodturning Projects	*Keith Rowley*	Woodturning Techniques	*GMC Publications*
Making Screw Threads in Wood	*Fred Holder*	*Woodturning* Tools & Equipment Test Reports	*GMC Publications*
Turned Boxes: 50 Designs	*Chris Stott*	Woodturning Wizardry	*David Springett*
Turning Green Wood	*Michael O'Donnell*		

Crafts

Gardening

Auriculas for Everyone: How to Grow and Show Perfect Plants
Mary Robinson

Beginners' Guide to Herb Gardening   Yvonne Cuthbertson

Bird Boxes and Feeders for the Garden   Dave Mackenzie

The Birdwatcher's Garden   Hazel & Pamela Johnson

Broad-Leaved Evergreens   Stephen G. Haw

Companions to Clematis: Growing Clematis with Other Plants
Marigold Badcock

Creating Contrast with Dark Plants   Freya Martin

Creating Small Habitats for Wildlife in your Garden   Josie Briggs

Exotics are Easy   GMC Publications

Gardening with Wild Plants   Julian Slatcher

Growing Cacti and Other Succulents in the Conservatory and
Indoors   Shirley-Anne Bell

Growing Cacti and Other Succulents in the Garden
Shirley-Anne Bell

Hardy Perennials: A Beginner's Guide   Eric Sawford

Hedges: Creating Screens and Edges   Averil Bedrich

The Living Tropical Greenhouse: Creating a Haven for Butterflies
John & Maureen Tampion

Orchids are Easy: A Beginner's Guide to their Care and Cultivation
Tom Gilland

Plant Alert: A Garden Guide for Parents   Catherine Collins

Planting Plans for Your Garden   Jenny Shukman

Plants that Span the Seasons   Roger Wilson

Sink and Container Gardening Using Dwarf Hardy Plants
Chris & Valerie Wheeler

The Successful Conservatory and Growing Exotic Plants   Joan Phelan

VIDEOS

Drop-in and Pinstuffed Seats   David James

Stuffover Upholstery   David James

Elliptical Turning   David Springett

Woodturning Wizardry   David Springett

Turning Between Centres: The Basics   Dennis White

Turning Bowls   Dennis White

Boxes, Goblets and Screw Threads   Dennis White

Novelties and Projects   Dennis White

Classic Profiles   Dennis White

Twists and Advanced Turning   Dennis White

Sharpening the Professional Way   Jim Kingshott

Sharpening Turning & Carving Tools   Jim Kingshott

Bowl Turning   John Jordan

Hollow Turning   John Jordan

Woodturning: A Foundation Course   Keith Rowley

Carving a Figure: The Female Form   Ray Gonzalez

The Router: A Beginner's Guide   Alan Goodsell

The Scroll Saw: A Beginner's Guide   John Burke

MAGAZINES

WOODTURNING ✦ WOODCARVING ✦ FURNITURE & CABINETMAKING
THE ROUTER ✦ WOODWORKING ✦ THE DOLLS' HOUSE MAGAZINE
WATER GARDENING ✦ EXOTIC GARDENING ✦ GARDEN CALENDAR
OUTDOOR PHOTOGRAPHY ✦ BLACK & WHITE PHOTOGRAPHY
BUSINESSMATTERS

The above represents a full list of all titles currently published or scheduled to be published.
All are available direct from the Publishers or through bookshops, newsagents and specialist retailers.
To place an order, or to obtain a complete catalogue, contact:

GMC Publications,
Castle Place, 166 High Street, Lewes, East Sussex BN7 1XU, United Kingdom
Tel: 01273 488005 Fax: 01273 478606
E-mail: pubs@thegmcgroup.com

Orders by credit card are accepted